R00008 75683

CHICAGO PUBLIC LIBRARY
HAROLD WASHINGTON LIBRARY CENTER

D1566868

THE LOVER'S TREASURY OF VERSE

THE HEART'S AWAKENING.

From painting by W. A. Bouguereau.

The Lovers' Treasury of Verse

Selected by
John White Chadwick
and
Annie Hathaway Chadwick

Illustrated

Granger Index Reprint Series

BOOKS FOR LIBRARIES PRESS
FREEPORT, NEW YORK

First Published 1891
Reprinted 1970

REF
PR1184
.C4
1970

cop. 1

INTERNATIONAL STANDARD BOOK NUMBER:
0-8369-6212-5

LIBRARY OF CONGRESS CATALOG CARD NUMBER:
70-139758

PRINTED IN THE UNITED STATES OF AMERICA

THE CHICAGO PUBLIC LIBRARY

OCT 11 1971 B

OUT OF THE HEART.

Out of the heart it came, the impulse strong,
With patient labor and with loving art
This wreath to gather, — every flower a song
      Out of the heart.

And some have morning's dew on every part;
And some have drunk the sunshine all day long;
And some are paler for love's secret smart.

Dear, happy children, who can do no wrong,
A few have brought; a few like tear-drops start,
For those whose treasure has been missing long,
      Out of the heart.

                              J. W. C.

NOTE.

IT is not without regret that we have omitted from our selection many beautiful examples in this kind which have the rank of classics in the lyric art. We have done it because they are so generally known and so easily accessible, especially in Palgrave's " Golden Treasury,"—the best of all anthologies. But we could not deny ourselves a few of these, nor a few of Shakspere's sonnets, where we craved a double score. We trust that our selection has the merits of freshness and genuine feeling and true poetry in the main. If personal considerations have included some not equal to these standards, the indulgence of the reader for them is herewith desired. Our deliberate gleanings, though near and far, have yielded us few poems in comparison with our happy memories of much-loved things. The little we have trenched on previous anthologies is justified by the lover's right of eminent domain.

While giving authors' names in full in the table of contents, we have with the separate poems sometimes used other forms when they have a more familiar sound. Our gratitude is due, and is hereby expressed, for the kindness of many authors and publishers in allowing us the use of their poems and their publications.

INDEX OF AUTHORS.

———◆———

LIST OF ILLUSTRATIONS

———◆———

THE LOVER'S TREASURY OF VERSE

EROS.

THE sense of the world is short, —
Long and various the report, —
To love and be beloved;
Men and gods have not outlearned it;
And, how oft soe'er they 've turned it,
'T is not to be improved.

RALPH WALDO EMERSON.

"OH, LOVE IS NOT A SUMMER MOOD."

OH, Love is not a summer mood,
Nor flying phantom of the brain,
Nor youthful fever of the blood,
Nor dream, nor fate, nor circumstance.
Love is not born of blinded chance,
Nor bred in simple ignorance.

Love is the flower of maidenhood;
Love is the fruit of mortal pain;
And she hath winter in her blood.

I

True love is steadfast as the skies,
And once alight she never flies;
And love is strong, and love is wise.

RICHARD WATSON GILDER.

THE FIRST MEETING.

I WISH I could remember that first day,
    First hour, first moment of your meeting me,
  If bright or dim the season, it might be
Summer or winter for aught I can say;
So unrecorded did it slip away,
    So blind was I to see and to foresee,
    So dull to mark the budding of my tree
That would not blossom yet for many a May.
If only I could recollect it — such
    A day of days !   I let it come and go
    As traceless as a thaw of bygone snow;
It seemed to mean so little, meant so much;
If only now I could recall that touch,
    First touch of hand in hand — did one but know !

CHRISTINA ROSSETTI.

SUMMUM BONUM.

ALL the breath and the bloom of the year in the
    bag of one bee:
  All the wonder and wealth of the mine in the heart
    of one gem:

In the core of one pearl all the shade and the shine
    of the sea :
  Breath and bloom, shade and shine,—wonder, wealth,
    and — how far above them —
        Truth, that's brighter than gem,
        Trust, that's purer than pearl, —
Brightest truth, purest trust in the universe — all were
    for me
        In the kiss of one girl.
                  Robert Browning.

WITH STRAWBERRIES.

WITH strawberries we filled a tray,
    And then we drove away, away
Along the links beside the sea,
Where wave and wind were light and free,
And August felt as fresh as May.

And where the springy turf was gay
With thyme and balm and many a spray
Of wild roses, you tempted me
             With strawberries.

A shadowy sail, silent and gray,
Stole like a ghost across the bay ;
But none could hear me ask my fee,
And none could know what came to be.
Can sweethearts *all* their thirst allay
             With strawberries ?
        William Ernest Henley.

THE GARDEN OF LOVE.

FROM you have I been absent in the spring,
  When proud-pied April dress'd in all his trim
Hath put a spirit of youth in everything,
That heavy Saturn laugh'd and leap'd with him.
Yet nor the lay of birds, nor the sweet smell
Of different flowers in odour and in hue,
Could make me any summer's story tell,
Or from their proud lap pluck them where they grew;
Nor did I wonder at the lily's white,
Nor praise the deep vermilion in the rose;
They were but sweet, but figures of delight,
Drawn after you, you pattern of all those.
Yet seem'd it winter still, and, you away,
As with your shadow I with these did play.

WILLIAM SHAKSPERE.

"I COUNT MY TIMES BY TIMES THAT I MEET THEE."

I COUNT my times by times that I meet thee;
  These are my yesterdays, my morrows, noons
  And nights; these my old moons and my new moons.
  Slow fly the hours, or fast the hours do flee,
If thou art far from or art near to me:
  If thou art far, the birds' tunes are no tunes;
  If thou art near, the wintry days are Junes, —
  Darkness is light, and sorrow cannot be.

Thou art my dream come true, and thou my dream,
  The air I breathe, the world wherein I dwell;
  My journey's end thou art, and thou the way;
Thou art what I would be, yet only seem;
  Thou art my heaven and thou art my hell;
  Thou art my ever-living judgment day.

              RICHARD WATSON GILDER.

WER WENIG SUCHT, DER FINDET VIEL.

Translated from Rückert.

ONLY a shelter for my head I sought,
  One stormy winter night;
To me the blessing of my life was brought,
  Making the whole world bright.
How shall I thank thee for a gift so sweet,
  O dearest Heavenly Friend?
I sought a resting-place for weary feet,
  And found my journey's end.

Only the latchet of a friendly door
  My timid fingers tried;
A loving heart, with all its precious store,
  To me was opened wide.
I asked for shelter from a passing shower, —
  My sun shall always shine!
I would have sat beside the hearth an hour, —
  And the whole heart was mine!

              LILIAN CLARKE.

THE QUEEN.

TO heroism and holiness
   How hard it is for man to soar,
But how much harder to be less
   Than what his mistress loves him for!
He does with ease what do he must,
   Or lose her, and there's nought debarr'd
From him who's call'd to meet her trust,
   And credit her desired regard.
Ah, wasteful woman, she that may
   On her sweet self set her own price,
Knowing he cannot choose but pay,
   How has she cheapen'd paradise;
How given for nought her priceless gift,
   How spoil'd the bread and spill'd the wine,
Which spent with due, respective thrift,
   Had made brutes men, and men divine!

O Queen, awake to thy renown,
   Require what 't is our wealth to give,
And comprehend and wear the crown
   Of thy despised prerogative!
I who in manhood's name at length
   With glad songs come to abdicate
The gross regality of strength,
   Must yet in this thy praise abate,
That through thine erring humbleness
   And disregard of thy degree,

Mainly, has man been so much less
    Than fits his fellowship with thee.
High thoughts had shaped the foolish brow,
    The coward had grasp'd the hero's sword,
The vilest had been great, hadst thou,
    Just to thyself, been worth's reward:
But lofty honours undersold
    Seller and buyer both disgrace ;
And favour that makes folly bold
    Puts out the light in virtue's face.

COVENTRY PATMORE.

LOVE AGAINST LOVE.

AS unto blowing roses summer dews,
    Or morning's amber to the tree-top choirs,
So to my bosom are the beams that use
    To rain on me from eyes that love inspires.
Your love, vouchsafe it, royal-hearted few,
    And I will set no common price thereon;
Oh! I will keep as heaven its holy blue,
    Or night her diamonds, that dear treasure won.
But aught of inward faith must I forego,
    Or miss one drop from Truth's baptismal hand,
Think poorer thoughts, pray cheaper prayers, and grow
    Less worthy trust, to meet your heart's demand?
Farewell! Your wish I for your sake deny;
Rebel to love in truth to love am I.

DAVID A. WASSON.

FULNESS OF LOVE.

IF I leave all for thee, wilt thou exchange
        And *be* all to me?   Shall I never miss
Home-talk and blessing, and the common kiss
That comes to each in turn, nor count it strange,
When I look up, to drop on a new range
Of walls and floors, . . . another home than this?
Nay, wilt thou fill that place by me which is
Filled by dead eyes too tender to know change?
That's hardest!   If to conquer love, has tried,
To conquer grief tries more . . . as all things prove,
For grief indeed is love and grief beside.
Alas, I have grieved so I am hard to love —
Yet love me — wilt thou?   Open thine heart wide,
And fold within the wet wings of thy dove.

                    ELIZABETH BARRETT BROWNING.

AT THE CHURCH GATE.

ALTHOUGH I enter not,
        Yet round about the spot
    Ofttimes I hover:
And near the sacred gate,
With longing eyes I wait,
    Expectant of her.

The Minster bell tolls out
Above the city's rout
 And noise and humming:
They 've hushed the Minster bell:
The organ 'gins to swell:
 She 's coming, she 's coming !

My lady comes at last,
Timid, and stepping fast,
 And hastening hither,
With modest eyes downcast:
She comes — she 's here — she 's past —
 May Heaven go with her !

Kneel, undisturb'd, fair Saint !
Pour out your praise or plaint
 Meekly and duly;
I will not enter there,
To sully your pure prayer
 With thoughts unruly.

But suffer me to pace
Round the forbidden place,
 Lingering a minute,
Like outcast spirits who wait
And see through heaven's gate
 Angels within it.

    WILLIAM M. THACKERAY.

PALABRAS CARIÑOSAS.

Spanish Air.

GOOD-NIGHT! I have to say good-night
   To such a host of peerless things!
Good-night unto that fragile hand
All queenly with its weight of rings;
Good-night to fond, uplifted eyes,
Good-night to chestnut braids of hair,
Good-night unto the perfect mouth,
And all the sweetness nestled there —
   The snowy hand detains me, then
   I 'll have to say Good-night again!

But there will come a time, my love,
When, if I read our stars aright,
I shall not linger by this porch
With my adieus.   Till then, good-night!
You wish the time were now?   And I.
You do not blush to wish it so?
You would have blushed yourself to death
To own so much a year ago —
   What, both these snowy hands!   Ah, then
   I 'll have to say Good-night again!

THOMAS BAILEY ALDRICH.

SILENT NOON.

YOUR hands lie open in the long fresh grass, —
　　The finger-points look through like rosy blooms :
　Your eyes smile peace.　The pasture gleams and
　　glooms
Neath billowing skies that scatter and amass.
All round our nest, far as the eye can pass,
　　Are golden kingcup-fields with silver edge
　　Where the cow-parsley skirts the hawthorn-hedge.
'T is visible silence, still as the hour-glass.

Deep in the sun-searched growths the dragon-fly
Hangs like a blue thread loosened from the sky : —
　　So this wing'd hour is dropt to us from above.
Oh ! clasp we to our hearts, for deathless dower,
This close-companioned inarticulate hour
　　When twofold silence was the song of love.

　　　　　　　　　　DANTE G. ROSSETTI.

A NICE CORRESPONDENT.

THE glow and the glory are plighted
　　To darkness, for evening is come ;
　The lamp in Glebe Cottage is lighted,
　　The birds and the sheep-bells are dumb.
I 'm alone, for the others have flitted
　　To dine with a neighbor at Kew ;
Alone, but I 'm not to be pitied —
　　　　　I 'm thinking of you !

I wish you were here! Were I duller
　　Than dull, you 'd be dearer than dear;
I am drest in your favourite colour —
　　Dear Fred, how I wish you were here!
I am wearing my lazuli necklace, —
　　The necklace you fastened askew!
Was there ever so rude and so reckless
　　　　　A darling as you?

I want you to come and pass sentence
　　On two or three books with a plot;
Of course you know "Janet's Repentance"?
　　I 'm reading Sir *Waverly* Scott,
That story of Edgar and Lucy,
　　How thrilling, romantic, and true!
The Master (his bride was a *goosey!*)
　　　　　Reminds me of you.

They tell me Cockaigne has been crowning
　　A Poet whose garland endures; —
It was you who first spouted me Browning, —
　　That stupid old Browning of yours!
His vogue and his verve are alarming,
　　I 'm anxious to give him his due,
But, Fred, he 's not nearly so charming
　　　　　A poet as you.

I heard how you shot at the Beeches,
　　I saw how you rode *Chanticleer*,
I have read the report of your speeches,
　　And echo'd the echoing cheer:

There 's a whisper of hearts you are breaking,
  Dear Fred, I believe it, I do!
Small marvel that Fashion is making
      Her idol of you!

Alas for the world, and its dearly
  Bought triumph, its fugitive bliss;
Sometimes I half wish I were merely
  A plain or a penniless miss ;
But perhaps one is best with " a measure
  Of pelf," and I 'm not sorry, too,
That I 'm pretty, because it 's a pleasure,
      My darling, to you !

Your whim is for frolic and fashion,
  Your taste is for letters and art; —
This rhyme is the common-place passion
  That glows in a fond woman's heart:
Lay it by in some sacred deposit
  For relics — we all have a few!
Love, some day they 'll print it, because it
      Was written to you.

                    FREDERICK LOCKER.

THE PROTEST.

I COULD not bear to see those eyes
  On all with wasteful largesse shine,
And that delight of welcome rise
Like sunshine strained through amber wine,

But that a glow from deeper skies,
From conscious fountains more divine,
Is (is it?) mine.

Be beautiful to all mankind,
As nature fashioned thee to be;
'T would anger me did all not find
The sweet perfection that's in thee:
Yet keep one charm of charms behind, —
Nay, thou 'rt so rich, keep two or three
For (is it?) me!

JAMES RUSSELL LOWELL.

FROM "MAUD."

QUEEN rose of the rosebud garden of girls,
    Come hither, the dances are done,
In gloss of satin and glimmer of pearls,
    Queen lily and rose in one;
Shine out, little head, sunning over with curls,
    To the flowers, and be their sun.

There has fallen a splendid tear
    From the passion-flower at the gate.
She is coming, my dove, my dear;
    She is coming, my life, my fate;
The red rose cries, "She is near, she is near;"
    And the white rose weeps, "She is late;"
The larkspur listens, "I hear, I hear;"
    And the lily whispers, "I wait."

She is coming, my own, my sweet;
 Were it ever so airy a tread,
My heart would hear her and beat,
 Were it earth in an earthy bed;
My dust would hear her and beat,
 Had I lain for a century dead;
Would start and tremble under her feet,
 And blossom in purple and red.

ALFRED TENNYSON.

LOVE'S MEANING.

I THOUGHT it meant all glad ecstatic things, —
 Fond glance and touch and speech, quick blood
 and brain,
And strong desire, and keen, delicious pain,
And beauty's thrall, and strange bewilderings
Twixt hope and fear, like to the little stings
 The rose-thorn gives, and then the utter gain —
 Worth all my sorest strivings to attain —
Of the dear bliss long-sought possession gives.

Now with a sad, clear sight that reassures
 My often sinking soul, with longing eyes
Averted from the path that still allures,
 Lest, seeing that for which my sore heart sighs,
I seek my own good at the cost of yours, —
 I know at last that love means sacrifice.

CARLOTTA PERRY.

SONG.

NOT from the whole wide world I chose thee —
    Sweetheart, light of the land and the sea!
The wide, wide world could not inclose thee,
    For thou art the whole wide world to me.

RICHARD WATSON GILDER.

THE WOMAN'S CAUSE.

THE woman's cause is man's : they rise or sink
    Together, dwarfed or godlike, bond or free :
For she that out of Lethe scales with man
The shining steps of Nature, shares with man
His nights, his days, moves with him to one goal,
Stays all the fair young planet in her hands —
If she be small, slight-natured, miserable,
How shall men grow ?   But work no more alone !
Our place is much ; as far as in us lies
We two will serve them both in aiding her, —
Will clear away the parasitic forms
That seem to keep her up, but drag her down ;
Will leave her space to burgeon out of all
Within her, — let her make herself her own
To give or keep, to live and learn and be
All that not harms distinctive womanhood.
For woman is not undeveloped man,
But diverse : could we make her as the man,
Sweet love were slain ; his dearest bond is this,

Not like to like, but like in difference:
Yet in the long years liker must they grow;
The man be more of woman, she of man;
He gain in sweetness and in moral height,
Nor lose the wrestling thews that throw the world;
She mental breadth, nor fail in childward care,
Nor lose the childlike in the larger mind;
Till at the last she set herself to man,
Like perfect music unto noble words;
And so these twain, upon the skirts of Time,
Sit side by side, full-summed in all their powers,
Dispensing harvest, sowing the To-be,
Self-reverent each, and reverencing each,
Distinct in individualities,
But like each other even as those who love.
Then comes the statelier Eden back to men;
Then reign the world's great bridals, chaste and calm;
Then springs the crowning race of humankind.
May these things be!

ALFRED TENNYSON.

WHEN LOVE MOST SECRET IS.

THE fountains smoke, and yet no flames they
    show;
  Stars shine by night, though undiscerned by day;
And trees do spring, yet are not seen to grow;
  And shadows move, although they seem to stay:
In Winter's woe is buried Summer's bliss,
And Love loves most when love most secret is.

The stillest streams descry the greatest deep;
  The clearest sky is subject to a shower;
Conceit's most sweet whenas it seems to sleep,
  And fairest days do in the morning lower:
The silent groves sweet nymphs they cannot miss,
For Love loves most when love most secret is.

The rarest jewels hidden virtue yield;
  The sweet of traffic is a secret gain;
The year once old doth show a barren field;
  And plants seem dead, and yet they spring again:
Cupid is blind; the reason why is this, —
Love loveth most when love most secret is.

ROBERT JONES: Elizabethan Song Book.

HAPPY INSENSIBILITY.

IN a drear-nighted December,
    Too happy, happy Tree,
Thy branches ne'er remember
    Their green felicity;
The north cannot undo them
With a sleety whistle through them,
Nor frozen thawings glue them
    From budding at the prime.

In a drear-nighted December,
    Too happy, happy Brook,
Thy bubblings ne'er remember
    Apollo's summer look;

But with a sweet forgetting
They stay their crystal fretting,
Never, never petting
   About the frozen time.

Ah, would 't were so with many
   A gentle girl and boy!
But were there ever any
   Writhed not at passèd joy?
To know the change and feel it,
When there is none to heal it,
Nor numbèd sense to steal it, —
   Was never said in rhyme.

JOHN KEATS.

MY MUSIC.

HOW oft, when thou, my music, music play'st,
   Upon that blessed wood whose motion sounds
With thy sweet fingers, when thou gently sway'st
The wiry concord that mine ear confounds,
Do I envy those jacks that nimble leap
To kiss the tender inward of thy hand,
Whilst my poor lips, which should that harvest reap,
At the wood's boldness by thee blushing stand!
To be so tickled, they would change their state
And situation with those dancing chips,
O'er whom thy fingers walk with gentle gait,
Making dead wood more blest than living lips.
Since saucy jacks so happy are in this,
Give them thy fingers, me thy lips to kiss.

WILLIAM SHAKSPERE.

STARLIGHT.

"LOOK up," she said; and all the heavens blazed
        With countless myriads of quiet stars,
Whereon a moment silently he gazed,
And drank that peace no trouble ever mars.
Then looking down into her face upturned,
Two other stars that did outshine the rest
Upward to him with such soft splendor yearned
That all her secret was at once confessed.
Then he with kisses did put out their light,
And said, "Oh, strange, but more, dear love, to me
Are thy pure eyes than all the stars of night
That shine in heaven everlastingly!
Night still is night, with every star aglow;
But light were night didst thou not love me so."

                              JOHN W. CHADWICK.

A NOBLER EXERCISE.

O KISSE, which doest those ruddie gemmes im-
        part,
Or gemmes or frutes of new-found Paradise,
Breathing all blisse, and sweet'ning to the heart,
Teaching dumbe lips a nobler exercise;
O kisse, which soules, even soules, together ties
By linkes of love and only Nature's art,
How faine would I paint thee to all men's eyes,
Or of thy gifts at least shade out some part!

But she forbids ; with blushing words she sayes
She builds her fame on higher-seated praise.
But my heart burnes; I cannot silent be.
Then, since, deare life, you faine would have me peace,
And I, mad with delight, want wit to cease,
Stop you my mouth with still, still kissing me.

SIR PHILIP SIDNEY.

THE MOTH'S KISS FIRST.

THE moth's kiss first !
    Kiss me as if you made believe
You were not sure, this eve,
How my face, your flower, had pursed
Its petals up ; so, here and there
You brush it, till I grow aware
Who wants me, and wide open burst.

The bee's kiss, now !
Kiss me as if you entered gay
My heart at some noonday, —
A bud that dares not disallow
The claim, so all is rendered up;
And passively its shattered cup
Over your head to sleep I bow.

ROBERT BROWNING.

AT LIFE'S BEST.

LOOK up, and let thy nature strike on mine
　　Like yonder morning on the blind half-world;
Approach and fear not; breathe upon my brows;
In that fine air I tremble, all the past
Melts mist-like into this bright hour, and this
Is morn to more, and all the rich to come
Reels, as the golden Autumn woodland reels
Athwart the smoke of burning weeds.　Forgive me,
I waste my heart in signs : let be.　My bride,
My wife, my life.　Oh, we will walk this world,
Yoked in all exercise of noble end,
And so through those dark gates across the wild
That no man knows.　Indeed I love thee; come,
Yield thyself up: my hopes and thine are one :
Accomplish thou my manhood and thyself,
Lay thy sweet hands in mine, and trust to me.

ALFRED TENNYSON.

LIFE IN A LOVE.

ESCAPE me ?
　　Never —
　　Beloved!
While I am I, and you are you,
　　So long as the world contains us both,
　　Me the loving and you the loth,
While the one eludes, must the other pursue.

My life is at fault at last I fear —
    It seems too much like a fate, indeed!
    Though I do my best, I shall scarce succeed;
But what if I fail of my purpose here?
It is but to keep the nerves at strain,
    To dry one's eyes and laugh at a fall,
And, baffled, get up to begin again, —
    So the chase takes up one's life, that's all.
While, look but once from your furthest bound,
    At me so deep in the dust and dark,
No sooner the old hope drops to ground
    Than a new one, straight to the self-same mark,
           I shape me —
           Ever
           Removed!
              Robert Browning.

LOVE IN A LIFE.

ROOM after room,
   I hunt the house through
We inhabit together.
Heart, fear nothing, for, heart, thou shalt find her,
Next time, herself! — not the trouble behind her
Left in the curtain, the couch's perfume!
As she brushed it, the cornice-wreath blossomed
    anew, —
Yon looking-glass gleamed at the wave of her feather.
Yet the day wears,
And door succeeds door;
I try the fresh fortune, —

Range the wide house from the wing to the centre.
Still the same chance! she goes out as I enter.
Spend my whole day in the quest, — who cares?
But 't is twilight, you see, — with such suites to explore,
Such closets to search, such alcoves to importune!

ROBERT BROWNING.

LOVE AND PRUDENCE.

D^O you remember that most perfect night,
    In the full flush of June,
When the wide heavens were tranced in silver light
    Of the sad, patient moon?
Silent we sat, awed by a strange unrest;
    The fathomless, far sky
Our very life absorbed, our thoughts oppressed,
    By its immensity.

Lost in that infinite vast, how idle seemed
    The best of human speech;
Earth scarcely breathed, so silently she dreamed,
    Save when from some far reach
The faint wind sighed, and stirred the slumbering
        trees,
    And shadowy stretch and plain
Seemed haunted by unuttered mysteries
    Night on its life had lain.

We knew not what we were, or where we went,
    Borne by some unseen power,

Nor in what dream-shaped realms our spirits spent
    That long, yet brief half-hour;
I only know that, as a star from high
    Slides down the ether thin,
We shot to earth, roused by a startling cry,
    " You 're getting cold, — come in."

WILLIAM WETMORE STORY.

THE AMULET.

YOUR picture smiles as first it smiled ;
    The ring you gave is still the same ;
Your letter tells, O changing child !
    No tidings *since* it came.

Give me an amulet
    That keeps intelligence with you, —
Red when you love, and rosier red,
    And when you love not, pale and blue.

Alas ! that neither bonds nor vows
    Can certify possession ;
Torments me still the fear that love
    Died in its last expression.

RALPH WALDO EMERSON.

RIDING DOWN.

OH, did you see him riding down,
    And riding down, while all the town
Came out to see, came out to see,
And all the bells rang mad with glee ?

Oh, did you hear those bells ring out,
The bells ring out, the people shout,
And did you hear that cheer on cheer
That over all the bells rang clear?

And did you see the waving flags,
The fluttering flags, the tattered flags,
Red, white, and blue, shot through and through,
Baptized with battle's deadly dew?

And did you hear the drum's gay beat,
The drum's gay beat, the bugles sweet,
The cymbals clash, the cannon's crash,
That rent the sky with sound and flash?

And did you see me waiting there,
Just waiting there and watching there, —
One little lass, amid the mass
That pressed to see the hero pass?

And did you see him smiling down,
And smiling down, as riding down
With slowest pace, with stately grace,
He caught the vision of a face, —

My face uplifted, red and white,
Turned red and white with sheer delight,
To meet the eyes, the smiling eyes,
Outflashing in their swift surprise?

Oh, did you see how swift it came,
How swift it came, like sudden flame,
That smile to me, to only me,
The little lass who blushed to see?

And at the windows all along,
Oh, all along, a lovely throng
Of faces fair, beyond compare,
Beamed out upon him riding there!

Each face was like a radiant gem,
A sparkling gem; and yet for them
No swift smile came, like sudden flame,
No arrowy glance took certain aim.

He turned away from all their grace;
From all that grace of perfect face,
He turned to me, to only me,
The little lass who blushed to see.

NORA PERRY.

ROMANY SONG.

IF I were your little baby,
  If you were my mother old,
You would give me a kiss, my darling, —
  "Oh, sir, you are far too bold."

But as you are not my mother,
  But as I am not your son,
Ah! that is another matter;
  So, may be, I'll give you one.

LELAND'S ANGLO-ROMANY SONGS.

LOVE.

WHEN daffodils began to blow,
   And apple-blossoms thick to snow
Upon the brown and breaking mould, —
'T was in the spring, — we kissed and sighed
And loved, and heaven and earth defied,
   We were so young and bold.

The fluttering bob-link dropped his song,
The first young swallow curved along,
   The daisy stared in sturdy pride,
When, loitering on, we plucked the flowers,
But dared not own those thoughts of ours
   Which yet we could not hide.

Tiptoe you bent the lilac spray
And shook its rain of dew away
   And reached it to me with a smile:
" Smell that, how full of spring it is " —
'T is now as full of memories
   As 't was of dew erewhile.

Your hand I took, to help you down
The broken wall, from stone to stone,
   Across the shallow bubbling brook.
Ah! what a thrill went from that palm,
That would not let my blood be calm,
   And through my pulses shook.

Often our eyes met as we turned,
And both our cheeks with passion burned,
    And both our hearts grew riotous,
Till, as we sat beneath the grove,
I kissed you — whispering, "We love" —
    As thus I do — and thus.

When passion had found utterance,
Our frightened hearts began to glance
    Into the Future's every day;
And how shall we our love conceal,
Or dare our passion to reveal, —
    "We are too young," they'll say.

Alas! we are not now too young,
Yet love to us hath safely clung,
    Despite of sorrow, years, and care —
But ah! we have not what we had,
We cannot be so free, so glad,
    So foolish as we were.

WILLIAM WETMORE STORY.

A PEARL — A GIRL.

A SIMPLE ring with a single stone,
    To the vulgar eye no stone of price:
Whisper the right word, — that alone, —
    Forth starts a sprite, like fire from ice,
And lo! you are lord (says an Eastern scroll)
Of heaven and earth, lord whole and sole,
    Through the power in a pearl.

A woman ('t is I this time that say),
    With little the world counts worthy praise :
Utter the true word, — out and away
    Escapes her soul : I am wrapt in blaze,
Creation's lord, of heaven and earth
Lord whole and sole — by a minute's birth,
    Through the love in a girl.

ROBERT BROWNING.

WHAT ELSE?

THEY walked together, in the dusk,
    Along the garden's shrubbery-edge ;
The heavy roses' scattered musk
    Blew faint across the cedar-hedge :
A spotted snake came gliding through : —
    To shield her from imagined harms,
What should he do, what *could* he do,
    But take her safe into his arms ?

While for one happy moment still
    Her head was leaning on his breast,
He felt a little tremor thrill
    The hand against his shoulder prest :
The parted lips were trembling too : —
    Some feeling for her fears to show,
What should he do, what *could* he do,
    But kiss her ere he let her go ?

Redder than in the garden bed
    The roses blossomed to her cheek :

SPRINGTIME OF LOVE.
From painting by Paul Thumann.

"You wicked, wicked cheat!" she said,
  Soon as the injured lips could speak.
Lest he should prove her charge for true,
  And seem the most depraved of men,
What should he do, what *could* he do,
  But give her back the kiss again?

KATE PUTNAM OSGOOD.

AMOR OMNIA VINCIT.

WHEN, in disgrace with fortune and men's eyes,
  I all alone beweep my outcast state
And trouble deaf heaven with my bootless cries
And look upon myself, and curse my fate.
Wishing me like to one more rich in hope,
Featured like him, like him with friends possess'd,
Desiring this man's art and that man's scope,
With what I most enjoy contented least;
Yet in these thoughts myself almost despising,
Haply I think on thee, — and then my state,
Like to the lark at break of day arising
From sullen earth, sings hymns at heaven's gate;
For thy sweet love remember'd such wealth brings
That then I scorn to change my state with kings.

WILLIAM SHAKSPERE.

EARLY LOVE.

AH! I remember well (and how can I
  But evermore remember well?) when first
Our flame began, when scarce we knew what was
The flame we felt; when as we sat and sighed

And looked upon each other, and conceived
Not what we ailed, yet something we did ail
And yet were well, and yet we were not well,
And what was our disease we could not tell.
Then would we kiss, then sigh, then look; and thus
In that first garden of our simpleness
We spent our childhood.   But when years began
To reap the fruit of knowledge, — ah, how then
Would she with sterner looks, with graver brow,
Check my presumption and my forwardness !
Yet still would give me flowers, still would show
What she would have me, yet not have me know.

SAMUEL DANIEL.

AN OLD LOVER.

HOW many new years have grown old
   Since first your servant old was new!
How many long hours have I told
   Since first my love was vowed to you !
And yet, alas ! she doth not know
Whether her servant love or no.

How many walls as white as snow,
   And windows clear as any glass,
Have I conjúred to tell you so,
   Which faithfully performed was !
And yet you 'll swear you do not know
Whether your servant love or no.

How often hath my pale lean face,
  With true charácters of my love,
Petitionéd to you for grace,
  Whom neither sighs nor tears can move!
O cruel, yet you do not know
Whether your servant love or no?

And wanting oft a better token,
  I have been fain to send my heart,
Which now your cold disdain hath broken,
  Nor can you heal 't by any art:
O look upon 't and you shall know
Whether your servant love or no.

ROBERT JONES: *Elizabethan Song Book.*

TOUJOURS AMOUR.

PRITHEE tell me, Dimple-Chin,
    At what age does Love begin?
Your blue eyes have scarcely seen
Summers three, my fairy queen,
But a miracle of sweets,
Soft approaches, sly retreats,
Show the little archer there,
Hidden in your pretty hair;
When didst learn a heart to win?
Prithee tell me, Dimple-Chin!

3

"Oh!" the rosy lips reply,
 "I can't tell you if I try.
'T is so long I can't remember:
 Ask some younger lass than I."

Tell, O tell me, Grizzled Face,
Do your heart and head keep pace?
When does hoary Love expire,
When do frosts put out the fire?
Can its embers burn below
All that chill December snow?
Care you still soft hands to press,
Bonny heads to smooth and bless?
When does Love give up the chase?
Tell, O tell me, Grizzled Face!

"Ah!" the wise old lips reply,
 "Youth may pass and strength may die;
But of Love I can't foretoken:
 Ask some older sage than I."

EDMUND CLARENCE STEDMAN.

LOVERS.

HE gather'd blue forget-me-nots,
  To fling them laughing on her knee.
She cried, "Ah, no; if thou canst go,
  Ah, love, thou shalt forgotten be!"

He gather'd golden buttercups,
   That grew so very fresh and free.
" Ah, happy plays, in childish days,
   When buttercups were gold to me ! "

He gather'd little meadow-sweet
   And hid it where she could not see.
She peeped about and found it out,
   And laugh'd aloud, and so did he.

He gather'd shining silver-weed ;
   He stole the heather from the bee :
Amid the grass the minutes pass,
   And twilight lingers on the lea.

ANON.

MY STAR.

ALL that I know
   Of a certain star,
Is, it can throw
   (Like the angled spar)
Now a dart of red,
   Now a dart of blue,
Till my friends have said
   They would fain see, too,
My star that dartles the red and the blue !
Then it stops like a bird, — like a flower, hangs furled ;
  They must solace themselves with the Saturn
    above it.
What matter to me if their star is a world ?
  Mine has opened its soul to me ; therefore I love it.

ROBERT BROWNING.

ANN HATHAWAY.

WOULD ye be taught, ye feathered throng,
    With love's sweet notes to grace your song
To pierce the heart with thrilling lay :
Listen to mine Ann Hathaway.
She hath a way to sing so clear,
Phœbus might wondering stop to hear.
To melt the sad, make blithe the gay ;
And Nature charm, Ann hath a way.
      She hath a way,
        Ann Hathaway ;
To breathe delight, Ann hath a way.

When envy's breath and rancorous tooth
Do soil and bite fair worth and truth,
And merit to distress betray :
To soothe the heart, Ann hath a way.
She hath a way to chase despair,
To heal all grief, to cure all care,
Turn foulest night to fairest day ;
Thou know'st, fond heart, Ann hath a way.
      She hath a way,
        Ann Hathaway ;
To make grief bliss, Ann hath a way.

Talk not of gems, the orient list,
The diamond, topaz, amethyst,
The emerald mild, the ruby gay ;
Talk of my gem, Ann Hathaway !

She hath a way, with her bright eye,
Their various lustre to defy, —
The jewels she, and the foil they,
So sweet to look, Ann hath a way,
     She hath a way,
     Ann Hathaway ;
To shame bright gems, Ann hath a way.

But were it to my fancy given
To rate her charms, I 'd call them heaven ;
For though a mortal made of clay,
Angels must love Ann Hathaway.
She hath a way so to control,
To rapture the imprisoned soul,
And sweetest heaven on earth display,
That to be heaven Ann hath a way.
     She hath a way,
     Ann Hathaway ;
To be heaven's self, Ann hath a way.

WILLIAM SHAKSPERE (?).

FATE.

ALL unconscious I beheld her ;
   Knew not that my fate was nigh, —
Fate that wears such various aspect
  To the victim's laughing eye.

Poets, painters, still to paint her
  Dark and gloomy do their best;
Were I painter, I would paint her
  All in cherry-color dressed.

She should be a little maiden,
  Modest, shrinking, sweet and fair,
At a party, playing forfeits,
  Looking, " Kiss me if you dare!"

Did I kiss you? If I did n't,
  'T was the blunder of my life.
Was the last the hundred millionth?
  Just one more then, little wife.

                    JOHN W. CHADWICK.

FATE.

A FACE of a summer ago,
    Of a maid I met by the sea,
Haunts me wherever I go,
    And is always looking at me
    With a curious constancy.

And whether I will it or no,
    I cannot get rid of her gaze,
Standing and looking so,
    With her modest and maidenly ways,
    And I would not the rest of my days.

                    MERLE ST. CROIX WRIGHT.

THE WHISPERING GALLERY.

SHE flushed and paled, and, bridling, raised her
   head:
  "How could you know that I was in distress,
  To come so far and timely with redress?
For well and close, I thought, I kept my dread
From common scorn or pity."
                "So?" he said,
"I scarce can tell, and yet it seems no less
Than that all circling winds and waters press
To bring me tidings how your life is led;

"And I could hear the whisper of your name
  Around the world.   If the whole earth should
  lie
Between us, and you fled when peril came,
  I'd feel your foot-beats throb, I think, and fly,
And come through sea or waste or battle-flame,
  And thank God's favor in your cause to die."

               JAMES T. McKAY.

TRANSLATION FROM HEINE.

THE letter which you wrote me
  Disturbs me not a whit;
You'll love no more, you tell me, —
  But there's too much of it.

Twelve pages, fine and neatly, —
　A little manuscript;
One writes not so completely
　When love's true knot is slipped.

MERLE ST. CROIX WRIGHT.

OF THREE GIRLS AND THEIR TALK.

BY a clear well, within a little field
　　Full of green grass and flowers of every hue,
　Sat three young girls, relating (as I knew)
Their loves. And each had twined a bough to shield
Her lovely face; and the green leaves did yield
　The golden hair their shadow; while the two
　Sweet colors mingled, both blown lightly through
With a soft wind forever stirred and still'd.
After a while one of them said,
　(I heard her,) "Think! If, ere the next hour struck,
　Each of our lovers should come here to-day,
Think you that we should fly, or feel afraid?"
　To whom the others answered, "From such luck
　A girl would be a fool to run away."

BOCCACCIO.

LOVE'S OMNIPRESENCE.

WERE I as base as is the lowly plain,
　　And you, my Love, as high as heaven above,
Yet should the thoughts of me, your humble swain,
Ascend to heaven, in honor of my Love.

Were I as high as heaven above the plain,
And you, my Love, as humble and as low
As are the deepest bottoms of the main,
Wheresoe'er you were, with you my Love should go.

Were you the earth, dear Love, and I the skies,
My love should shine on you like to the sun,
And look upon you with ten thousand eyes
Till heaven waxed blind, and till the world were done.

Wheresoe'er I am, below, or else above you,
Wheresoe'er you are, my heart shall truly love you.

JOSHUA SYLVESTER.

A MYSTERY.

THE love wherewith my heart is big for thee,
    Hath found no home with cowards or with
      slaves ;
It blooms a deathless flower among the free,
   And on untrodden heights unbroken waves.

No little heart can hold it, for it springs
   Twinned with eternity and scorn of death,
Feeding on hopes and high imaginings
   That fail not with our fitful human breath.

With those sweet strivings of the blood that stir
   Our souls in youth, and make our manhood great,
By interchange of love and life with her
   Who clings to us in bonds of equal fate,

This passion hath no part — nor on the roots
  Of sense and yearning stationed, nor upborne
By tenderness; nor are its sterner fruits
  Shown in dear kisses given at night or morn.

Be it enough that thou and I are one,
  That years and days seem nothing in the shine
Of that perpetual and unsinking sun
  Which nerves our souls with energy divine.

If tongue might tell the mystery I mean,
  Then all the world would love perchance like us ;
But should these lines by the great world be seen,
  They 'd move mere laughter.   Well : 't is better thus.

JOHN ADDINGTON SYMONDS.

THE DIFFICULTY.

TRANSLATED FROM HEINE.

ABOUT my Darling's lovely eyes
  I 've made no end of verses ;
About her precious little mouth,
Songs, which each voice rehearses ;
About my Darling's little cheek,
I wrote a splendid sonnet ;
And, — if she only had a heart,
I 'd write an ode upon it.

JAMES FREEMAN CLARKE.

RUTH.

SHE stood breast-high amid the corn,
    Clasped by the golden light of morn,
Like the sweetheart of the sun,
Who many a glowing kiss had won.

On her cheek an autumn flush,
Deeply ripened ; — such a blush
In the midst of brown was born,
Like red poppies grown with corn.

Round her eyes her tresses fell,
Which were blackest none could tell ;
But long lashes veiled a light
That had else been all too bright.

And her hat, with shady brim,
Made her tressy forehead dim ;
Thus she stood amid the stooks,
Praising God with sweetest looks.

" Sure," I said, " Heaven did not mean
Where I reap thou shouldst but glean ;
Lay thy sheaf adown and come,
Share my harvest and my home."

THOMAS HOOD.

HOW MANY TIMES.

HOW many times do I love thee, dear?
　　Tell me how many thoughts there be
　　　In the atmosphere
　　　Of a new-fallen year,
　　Whose white and sable hours appear
　　　The latest flake of Eternity:
So many times do I love thee, dear.

How many times do I love, again?
　　Tell me how many beads there are
　　　In a silver chain
　　　Of the evening rain,
　　Unravelled from the tumbling main,
　　　And threading the eye of a yellow star:
So many times do I love, again.

　　　　　　　　THOMAS LOVELL BEDDOES.

ASK ME NO MORE.

ASK me no more : the moon may draw the sea;
　　The cloud may stoop from heaven and take the
　　　shape,
　With fold to fold, of mountain or of cape;
But, O too fond, when have I answered thee?
　　Ask me no more.

MENU DE L'AMOUR.

From painting by Jean Aubert.

Ask me no more: what answer should I give?
  I love not hollow cheek or faded eye :
  Yet, O my friend, I will not have thee die !
Ask me no more, lest I should bid thee live ;
        Ask me no more.

Ask me no more : thy fate and mine are sealed :
  I strove against the stream, and all in vain :
  Let the great river take me to the main :
No more, dear love, for at a touch I yield ;
        Ask me no more.
              ALFRED TENNYSON.

KISSING HER HAIR.

KISSING her hair, I sat against her feet:
  Wove and unwove it, — wound and found it
    sweet;
Made fast therewith her hands, drew down her eyes,
Deep as deep flowers, and dreamy like dim skies;
With her own tresses bound, and found her fair, —
        Kissing her hair.

Sleep were no sweeter than her face to me, —
Sleep of cold sea-bloom under the cold sea :
What pain could get between my face and hers?
What new sweet thing would Love not relish worse ?
Unless perhaps white death has kissed me there, —
        Kissing her hair.
      ALGERNON CHARLES SWINBURNE.

ONE WORD IS TOO OFTEN PROFANED.

ONE word is too often profaned
    For me to profane it,
One feeling too falsely disdain'd
    For thee to disdain it.
One hope is too like despair
    For prudence to smother,
And Pity from thee more dear
    Than that from another.

I can give not what men call love,
    But wilt thou accept not
The worship the heart lifts above
    And the heavens reject not:
The desire of the moth for the star,
    Of the night for the morrow,
The devotion to something afar
    From the sphere of our sorrow?

             PERCY BYSSHE SHELLEY.

"LOVE DOTH TO HER EYES REPAIR."

Translated from Rückert.

WHY ask of others what they cannot say, —
    Others, who for thy good have little care?
Come close, dear friend, and learn a better way;
    Look in my eyes, and read my story there!

Trust not thine own proud wit; 't is idle dreaming !
  The common gossip of the street forbear ;
Nor even trust my acts or surface seeming :
  Ask only of my eyes ; my truth is there.

My lips refuse an answer to thy boldness ;
  Or with false, cruel words deny thy prayer, —
Believe them not, I hate them for their coldness !
  Look in my eyes ; my love is written there.

JAMES FREEMAN CLARKE

THE HAPPIEST GIRL IN THE WORLD.[1]

A WEEK ago ; and I am almost glad
    to have him now gone for this little while,
that I may think of him and tell myself
what to be his means, now that I am his,
and know if mine is love enough for him,
and make myself believe it all is true.

A week ago ; and it seems like a life,
and I have not yet learned to know myself :
I am so other than I was, so strange,
grown younger and grown older all in one ;
and I am not so sad and not so gay ;
and I think nothing, only hear him think.

And did I love him from the day we met ?
but I more gladly danced with some one else

---

[1] Parts of a poem.   The peculiar printing is preserved.

who waltzed more smoothly and was merrier:
and did I love him when he first came here?
but I more gladly talked with some one else
whose words were readier and who sought me more.
When did I love? How did it begin?

Ah, well, I would that I could love him more,
and not be only happy as I am;
I would that I could love him to his worth,
with that forgetting all myself in him,
that subtle pain of exquisite excess,
that momentary infinite sharp joy,
I know by books but cannot teach my heart:
and yet I think my love must needs be love,
since he can read me through — oh happy strange,
my thoughts that were my secrets all for me
grown instantly his open easy book! —
since he can read me through, and is content.

And shall I for so many coming days
be flower and sweetness to him? O pale flower,
grow, grow, and blossom out, and fill the air,
feed on his richness, grow, grow, blossom out,
and fill the air, and be enough for him.

My love, my love, my love! And I shall be
so much to him, so almost everything:
and I shall be the friend whom he will trust,
and I shall be the child whom he will teach,
and I shall be the servant he will praise,

and I shall be the mistress he will love,
and I shall be his wife.   O days to come,
will ye not pass like gentle rhythmic steps
that fall to sweetest music noiselessly?

Together always, that was what he said ;
together always.   O dear coming days !
O dear dear present days that pass too fast,
although they bring such rainbow morrows on !
that pass so fast, and yet, I know not why,
seem always to encompass so much time.
And I should fear I were too happy now,
and making this poor world too much my Heaven,
but that I feel God nearer, and it seems
as if I had learned His love better too.

AUGUSTA WEBSTER.

HIS LADY'S PRAISE.

MY lady carries love within her eyes;
    All that she looks on is made pleasanter;
  Upon her path men turn to gaze at her;
He whom she greeteth feels his heart to rise,
And droops his troubled visage, full of sighs,
  And of his evil heart is then aware :
  Hate loves, and pride becomes a worshipper.
O women, help to praise her in somewise.
Humbleness, and the hope that hopeth well,
  By speech of hers into the mind are brought,

4

And who beholds is blessèd oftenwhiles,
The look she hath when she a little smiles
Cannot be said, nor holden in the thought;
'T is such a new and generous miracle.

DANTE: *Vita Nuova*

PRISCILLA.

MY little Love sits in the shade
   Beneath the climbing roses,
And gravely sews in a half-dream
The dainty measures of her seam
   Until the twilight closes.

I look and long, yet have no care
   To break her maiden musing;
I idly toss my book away,
And watch the pretty fingers stray
   Along their task confusing.

The dews fall, and the sunset light
   Goes creeping o'er the meadows,
And still, with serious eyes cast down,
She gravely sews her wedding-gown
   Among the growing shadows.

I needs must gaze, though on her cheek
   The bashful roses quiver —
She is so modest, simple, sweet,
That I, poor pilgrim, at her feet
   Would fain adore forever.

A heavenly peace dwells in her heart ;
 Her love is yet half duty,
Serene and serious, still and quaint,
She 's partly woman, partly saint,
 This Presbyterian beauty.

She is so shy that all my prayers
 Scarce win a few small kisses —
She lifts her lovely eyes to mine
And softly grants, with blush divine,
 Such slender grace as this is.

I watch her with a tender care
 And joy not free from sadness —
For what am I that I should take
This gentle soul and think to make
 Its future days all gladness ?

Can I fulfil those maiden dreams
 In some imperfect fashion ?
I am no hero, but I know
I love you, Dear — the rest I throw
 Upon your sweet compassion.

ELLEN MACKAY HUTCHINSON

"HAVE YOU GOT A BROOK IN YOUR LITTLE HEART?"

HAVE you got a brook in your little heart,
 Where bashful flowers blow,
And blushing birds go down to drink,
And shadows tremble so ?

And nobody knows, so still it flows,
That any brook is there;
And yet your little draught of life
Is daily drunken there.

Then look out for the little brook in March,
When the rivers overflow,
And the snows come hurrying from the hills,
And the bridges often go.

And later, in August it may be,
When the meadows parching lie,
Beware, lest this little brook of life
Some burning noon go dry!

EMILY DICKINSON.

MINE.

O HOW my heart is beating as her name I keep
    repeating,
    And I drink up joy like wine:
O how my heart is beating as her name I keep
    repeating,
    For the lovely girl is mine!
She's rich, she's fair, beyond compare,
Of noble mind, serene and kind —
And how my heart is beating as her name I keep
    repeating,
    For the lovely girl is mine.

O how my heart is beating as her name I keep
    repeating,
    In a music soft and fine ;
O how my heart is beating as her name I keep
    repeating,
    For the girl I love is mine.
She owns no lands, has no white hands,
Her lot is poor, her life obscure ; —
Yet how my heart is beating as her name I keep
    repeating,
    For the girl I love is mine.

DINAH MULOCK CRAIK.

DITTY.

MY true love hath my heart and I have his,
    By just exchange one to the other given :
I hold his dear, and mine he cannot miss ;
There never was a better bargain driven !
    My true love hath my heart, and I have his.

His heart in me keeps him and me in one,
My heart in him his thoughts and senses guides :
He loves my heart, for once it was his own,
I cherish his because in me it bides :
    My true love hath my heart, and I have his.

SIR PHILIP SIDNEY.

THE DIFFERENCE.

IT is the season now to go
　About the country high and low,
Among the lilacs hand in hand,
And two by two in fairy land.

The brooding boy, the sighing maid,
Wholly fain and half afraid,
Now meet along the hazel'd brook
To pass and linger, pause and look.

A year ago, and blithely paired,
Their rough-and-tumble play they shared;
They kissed and quarrelled, laughed and cried,
A year ago at Eastertide.

With bursting heart, with fiery face,
She strove against him in the race;
He unabashed her garter saw,
That now would touch her skirts with awe.

Now by the stile ablaze she stops,
And his demurer eyes he drops;
Now they exchange averted sighs,
Or stand and marry silent eyes.

And he to her a hero is,
And sweeter she than primroses;
Their common silence dearer far
Than nightingale and mavis are.

Now when they sever wedded hands,
Joy trembles in their bosom-strands,
And lovely laughter leaps and falls
Upon their lips in madrigals.

ROBERT LOUIS STEVENSON.

A PLEASANT SONG.

THE nightingale has a lyre of gold,
　　The lark's is a clarion call,
And the blackbird plays but a boxwood flute,
　　But I love him best of all.

For his song is all of the joy of life,
　　And we, in the mad spring weather,
We two have listened till he sang
　　Our hearts and lips together.

WILLIAM ERNEST HENLEY.

A RING POSY.

JESS and Jill are pretty girls,
　　Plump and well to do,
In a cloud of windy curls :
　　Yet I know who
Loves me more than curls or pearls.

I 'm not pretty, not a bit ;
　　Thin and sallow-pale ;
When I trudge along the street
　　I don't need a veil ;
Yet I have one fancy hit.

Jess and Jill can trill and sing
    With a flute-like voice,
Dance as light as bird on wing,
    Laugh for careless joys:
Yet 't is I who wear the ring.

Jess and Jill will mate some day,
    Surely, surely;
Ripen on to June through May,
While the sun shines make their hay,
    Slacken steps demurely:
Yet even there I lead the way.

CHRISTINA G. ROSSETTI.

"MY LOVE FOR THEE DOTH MARCH LIKE ARMED MEN."

MY love for thee doth march like armèd men
    Against a queenly city they would take.
Along the army's front its banners shake;
    Across the mountain and the sun-smit plain
It stedfast sweeps as sweeps the stedfast rain;
    And now the trumpet makes the still air quake,
    And now the thundering cannon doth awake
    Echo on echo, echoing loud again.
But, lo! the conquest higher than bard had sung;
    Instead of answering cannon comes a small
    White flag; the iron gates are open flung,
And flowers along the invaders' pathway fall.
    The city's conquerors feast their foes among,
    And their brave flags are trophies on her wall.

RICHARD WATSON GILDER.

THE WAYS OF LOVE.

HOW do I love thee? Let me count the ways.
  I love thee to the depth and breadth and height
My soul can reach, when feeling out of sight
For the ends of Being and Ideal Grace.
I love thee to the level of every day's
Most quiet need, by sun and candlelight.
I love thee freely, as men strive for Right;
I love thee purely, as they turn from Praise;
I love thee with the passion put to use
In my old griefs, and with my childhood's faith;
I love thee with a love I seemed to lose
With my lost saints, — I love thee with the breath,
Smiles, tears, of all my life ! — and, if God choose,
I shall but love thee better after death.

                        ELIZABETH BARRETT BROWNING.

IN THE YEAR THAT'S COME AND GONE.

IN the year that 's come and gone, love, his flying
  feather
Stooping slowly, gave us heart, and bade us walk
  together.
In the year that 's coming on, though many a troth be
  broken,
We at least will not forget aught that love hath spoken.

In the year that's come and gone, dear, we wove a
tether
All of gracious words and thoughts, binding two
together.
In the year that's coming on, with its wealth of roses,
We shall weave it stronger yet, ere the circle closes.

In the year that's come and gone, in the golden
weather,
Sweet, my sweet, we swore to keep the watch of life
together.
In the year that's coming on, rich in joy and sorrow,
We shall light our lamp, and wait life's mysterious
morrow.

WILLIAM ERNEST HENLEY.

LOVE'S VICTORY.

TWICE had the changing seasons run their round,
Bringing to mortals happiness and tears;
The third year came, and with it heaven itself
Took wing to fold its pinions on my heart!
Then in the self-same eyes I gazed again,
To read there love, immeasurable love,
In sanctity of virgin scripture writ;
And words were murmured, words that passed her lips
To pass again no others, but one breast
Still echoes with them, as with rolling hymns
And hallelujahs some high-vaulted roof,
Beneath which joy in praise its wealth outpours.

Then, as high-rising tides might lift a barque,
That long had waited, and the mariners,
Now homeward bound, with many a loud huzza,
Run to the ropes together, all as one
Lay hold, spread topsail and topgallant, set
The royals, fix the booms, while every soul
Bubbles with pleasure as before the prow
The gamesome foam goes dancing, and the wake
Grows white behind: so love and love's delight
Swelled to uplift me on their wide expanse,
While all the winds of promise blew me home.
And when the ocean of that summer's joy
Beat on the shores of autumn, then, there came
My heart to port, with all its argosies
Of hopes that furled their sails in blessedness.
Nor yet I called her *mine.* How could I dare?
Mine as the sky the eagle's, when he floats
Amid its deeps! Mine as the sun of June
Is propertied by the cup he paints with gold,
Or morning by the birds, whose folded sleep
Her soft ray touches till it flower in song!

DAVID A. WASSON.

FAR, AND YET NEAR.

GO from me. Yet I feel that I shall stand
Hence forward in thy shadow. Nevermore
Alone upon the threshold of my door
Of individual life, I shall command

The uses of my soul, nor lift my hand
Serenely in the sunshine as before,
Without the sense of that which I forbore, . .
Thy touch upon the palm. The widest land
Doom takes to part us, leaves thy heart in mine
With pulses that beat double. What I do
And what I dream include thee, as the wine
Must taste of its own grapes. And when I sue
God for myself, He hears that name of thine,
And sees within my eyes, the tears of two.

ELIZABETH BARRETT BROWNING.

BY THE SWINGING SEAS.

SHE sauntered by the swinging seas,
   A jewel glittered at her ear,
And, teasing her along, the breeze
   Brought many a rounded grace more near.

So passing, one with wave and beam,
   She left, for memory to caress,
A laughing thought, a golden gleam,
   A hint of hidden loveliness.

WILLIAM ERNEST HENLEY.

"LAST NIGHT IN BLUE MY LITTLE LOVE WAS DRESSED."

L AST night in blue my little love was dressed;
  And as she walked the room in maiden grace,
I looked into her fair and smiling face,
And said that blue became my darling best.
But when, this morn, a spotless virgin vest
  And robe of white did the blue one displace,
  She seemed a pearl-tinged cloud, and I was — space!
She filled my soul as cloud shapes fill the West.

And so it is that, changing day by day, —
  Changing her robe, but not her loveliness, —
Whether the gown be blue, or white, or gray,
  I deem that one her most becoming dress.
The truth is this : In any robe or way,
  I love her just the same, and cannot love her less!

CHARLES HENRY WEBB ("JOHN PAUL").

TO A GIRL.

T HOU art so very sweet and fair,
  With such a heaven in thine eyes,
It almost seems an overcare
  To ask thee to be good or wise.

As if a little bird were blam'd
  Because its song unthinking flows;
As if a rose should be asham'd
  Of being nothing but a rose.

ANON.

AGRO-DOLCE.

ONE kiss from all others prevents me,
  And sets all my pulses astir,
And burns on my lips and torments me:
  'T is the kiss that I fain would give her.

One kiss for all others requites me,
  Although it is never to be,
And sweetens my dreams and invites me:
  'T is the kiss that she dare not give me.

JAMES RUSSELL LOWELL.

CAPRICE.

SHE hung the cage at the window:
  " If he goes by," she said,
" He will hear my robin singing,
  And when he lifts his head,
I shall be sitting here to sew,
And he will bow to me I know."

The robin sang a love-sweet song,
  The young man raised his head;
The maiden turned away and blushed:
  " I am a fool ! " she said,
And went on broidering in silk
A pink-eyed rabbit, white as milk.

The young man loitered slowly
  By the house three times that day;
She took the bird from the window:
  " He need not look this way."
She sat at her piano long,
And sighed, and played a death-sad song.

But when the day was done, she said,
  " I wish that he would come!
Remember, Mary, if he calls
  To-night — I 'm not at home."
So when he rang, she went — the elf! —
She went and let him in herself.

They sang full long together
  Their songs love-sweet, death-sad;
The robin woke from his slumber,
  And rang out, clear and glad.
" Now go!" she coldly said; " 't is late;"
And followed him — to latch the gate.

He took the rosebud from her hair,
  While "You shall not!" she said;
He closed her hand within his own,
  And, while her tongue forbade,
Her will was darkened in the eclipse
Of blinding love upon his lips.

                    WILLIAM D. HOWELLS.

EVE'S DAUGHTER.

I WAITED in the little sunny room :
    The cool breeze waved the window-lace, at play,
The white rose on the porch was all in bloom,
    And out upon the bay
I watched the wheeling sea-birds go and come.

" Such an old friend, — she would not make me stay
    While she bound up her hair."   I turned, and lo,
Danaë in her shower ! and fit to slay
    All a man's hoarded prudence at a blow :
Gold hair, that streamed away
    As round some nymph a sunlit fountain's flow.

" She would not make me wait ! " but well I know
    She took a good half-hour to loose and lay
Those locks in dazzling disarrangement so !

EDWARD ROWLAND SILL.

ST. GEORGE'S, HANOVER SQUARE.

SHE pass'd up the aisle on the arm of her sire,
    A delicate lady in bridal attire,
    Fair emblem of virgin simplicity ;
Half London was there, and, my word, there were few
That stood by the altar, or hid in a pew,
    But envied Lord Nigel's felicity.

Beautiful bride! So meek in thy splendor,
So frank in thy love, and its trusting surrender,
    Departing you leave us the town dim!
May happiness wing to thy bower, unsought,
And may Nigel, esteeming his bliss as he ought,
    Prove worthy thy worship, — confound him!

FREDERICK LOCKER.

THE LOVE-LETTER.

WARMED by her hand and shadowed by her hair
        As close she leaned and poured her heart
            through thee,
    Whereof the articulate throbs accompany
The smooth black stream that makes thy whiteness
        fair, —
Sweet fluttering sheet, even of her breath aware, —
    Oh let thy silent song disclose to me
    That soul wherewith her lips and eyes agree
Like married music in Love's answering air.

Fain had I watched her when, at some fond thought,
    Her bosom to the writing closelier press'd,
    And her breast's secrets peered into her breast;
When, through eyes raised an instant, her soul sought
My soul, and from the sudden confluence caught
        The words that made her love the loveliest.

DANTE G. ROSSETTI.

5

SUMMER IS COMING.

" SUMMER is coming, summer is coming.
     I know it, I know it, I know it.
Light again, leaf again, life again, love again,"
     Yes, my wild little Poet.

Sing the new year in under the blue.
     Last year you sang it as gladly.
" New, new, new, new!"   Is it then *so* new
     That you should carol so madly?

" Love again, song again, nest again, young again!"
     Never a prophet so crazy!
And hardly a daisy as yet, little friend,
     See, there is hardly a daisy.

" Here again, here, here, here, happy year!"
     O warble unchidden, unbidden!
Summer is coming, is coming, my dear,
     And all the winters are hidden.

ALFRED TENNYSON.

UMPIRES.

WE chose our blossoms, sitting on the grass;
     His, Marguerites, with sunny, winsome faces,
Mine, the bright clover, with its statelier graces.
" Let these decide the argument, my lass;

FOND RECOLLECTIONS.

From painting by E. Niczky.

We 'll watch," said he, "the light-winged breezes pass
   And note which first the earliest whiff displaces :
   If it be daisy, yours the sore disgrace is,
And if it 's clover, then I yield, alas ! "
The lightsome quarrel was but half in jest ;
I would go homeward ; he would sit and rest —
The foolish cousin whom I would not wed.
Smiling we waited ; not a word we said,
In earnest he, and I quite debonair —
But oh, the stillness of that summer air !

So still it was — so still with quiet heat,
   The blossom lately from the brooklet quaffing
   Ceased its brisk dipping and sly telegraphing,
And scorned the blossom opposite to greet.
The very grass stood breathless at our feet ;
   When suddenly, our weighty silence chaffing,
   The leaves around broke out in muffled laughing,
And something stirred the fickle Marguerite !
   "Your flower," I cried. — "Ah, now it bends quite
      over ! "
   "Oho !" he answered — "see your nodding clover ! "
In truth, those silly blossoms fluttered so,
I really knew not if to stay or go. —
And so it happened that the twilight found me
Still resting there, — and Charley's arm around me.

                        MARY MAPES DODGE.

IN THREE DAYS.

SO, I shall see her in three days
    And just one night, but nights are short,
Then two long hours, and that is morn.
See how I come, unchanged, unworn —
Feel, where my life broke off from thine,
How fresh the splinters keep and fine, —
Only a touch and we combine!

Too long, this time of year, the days!
But nights — at least the nights are short.
As night shows where her one moon is,
A hand's-breadth of pure light and bliss,
So, life's night gives my lady birth
And my eyes hold her! what is worth
The rest of heaven, the rest of earth?

O loaded curls, release your store
Of warmth and scent as once before
The tingling hair did, lights and darks
Out-breaking into fairy sparks
When under curl and curl I pried
After the warmth and scent inside,
Thro' lights and darks how manifold —
The dark inspired, the light controlled!
As early Art embrowned the gold.

What great fear — should one say, "Three days
That change the world, might change as well

Your fortune; and if joy delays,
Be happy that no worse befell."
What small fear — if another says,
" Three days and one short night beside
May throw no shadow on your ways;
But years must teem with change untried,
With chance not easily defied,
With an end somewhere undescried."
No fear! — or if a fear be born
This minute, it dies out in scorn.
Fear? I shall see her in three days
And one night, now the nights are short,
Then just two hours, and that is morn.

ROBERT BROWNING.

"IF YOU WERE COMING IN THE FALL."

I F you were coming in the fall,
   I 'd brush the summer by
With half a smile and half a spurn,
   As housewives do a fly.

If I could see you in a year,
   I 'd wind the months in balls,
And put them each in separate drawers,
   Until their time befalls.

If only centuries delayed,
   I 'd count them on my hand,
Subtracting till my fingers dropped
   Into Van Diemen's land.

If certain, when this life was out,
   That yours and mine should be,
I 'd toss it yonder like a rind,
   And taste eternity.

But now, all ignorant of the length
   Of time's uncertain wing,
It goads me, like the goblin bee
   That will not state its sting.

EMILY DICKINSON.

"LOVE ME NOT, LOVE, FOR THAT I FIRST LOVED THEE."

LOVE me not, Love, for that I first loved thee,
   Nor love me, Love, for thy sweet pity's sake,
In knowledge of the mortal pain and ache
Which is the fruit of love's blood-veinéd tree.
Let others for my love give love to me:
   From other souls, oh, gladly will I take,
   This burning, heart dry thirst of love to slake,
What seas of human pity there may be!
Nay, nay, I care no more how love may grow,
   So that I hear thee answer to my call!
   Love me because my piteous tears do flow,
Or that my love for thee did first befall.
   Love me or late or early, fast or slow:
   But love me, Love, for love is one and all!

RICHARD WATSON GILDER.

TO THE VIRGINS, TO MAKE MUCH OF TIME.

GATHER ye rosebuds while ye may,
   Old time is still a-flying :
And this same flower that smiles to-day,
   To-morrow will be dying.

The glorious lamp of heaven, the sun,
   The higher he 's a getting,
The sooner will his race be run,
   And nearer he 's to setting.

That age is best which is the first,
   When youth and blood are warmer;
But being spent, the worse and worst
   Times still succeed the former.

Then be not coy, but use your time,
   And while ye may, go marry;
For having lost but once your prime,
   You may forever tarry.

ROBERT HERRICK.

THE PREGNANT COMMENT.

OPENING one day a book of mine,
   I absent, Hester found a line
Praised with a pencil mark, and this
She left transfigured with a kiss.

When next upon the page I chance,
Like Poussin's nymphs my pulses dance,
And whirl my fancy where it sees
Pan piping 'neath Arcàdian trees,
Whose leaves no winter-scenes rehearse,
Still young and glad as Homer's verse.
"What mean," I ask, "these sudden joys?
This feeling fresher than a boy's?
What makes this line, familiar long,
New as the first bird's April song?
I could, with sense illumined thus,
Clear doubtful texts in Æschylus!"

Laughing, one day she gave the key,
My riddle's open sesame;
Then added, with a smile demure,
Whose downcast lids veiled triumph sure,
"If what I left there give you pain,
You — you — can take it off again;
'T was for *my* poet, not for him,
Your Doctor Donne there!"

                              Earth grew dim
And wavered in a golden mist,
As rose, not paper leaves I kissed.
Donne, you forgive? I let you keep
Her precious comment, poet deep.

                    JAMES RUSSELL LOWELL.

FIRST, SECOND, THIRD.

FIRST time he kissed me, he but only kissed
   The fingers of this hand wherewith I write,
And ever since it grew more clean and white,
Slow to world-greetings,... quick with its "Oh list,"...
When the angels speak.   A ring of Amethyst
I could not wear here plainer to my sight
Than that first kiss.   The second passed in height
The first, and sought the forehead, and half missed,
Half falling on the hair, O beyond meed!
That was the chrism of love, which love's own crown,
With sanctifying sweetness, did precede.
The third upon my lips was folded down
In perfect, purple state! since when, indeed,
I have been proud, and said, " My Love, my own."

                    ELIZABETH BARRETT BROWNING.

HER PERFECT PRAISE.

THERE 'S a woman like a dew-drop, she 's so purer
   than the purest ;
And her noble heart 's the noblest, yes, and her sure
      faith 's the surest:
And her eyes are dark and humid, like the depth on
      depth of lustre
Hid i' the harebell, while her tresses, sunnier than the
   wild grape cluster,

Gush in golden-tinted plenty down her neck's rose-
 misted marble:
Then her voice 's music . . . call it the well's bubbling,
 the bird's warble!

And this woman says, " My days were sunless and my
 nights were moonless,
Parched the pleasant April herbage, and the lark's
 heart's outbreak tuneless,
If you loved me not! " And I who — (ah, for words
 of flame!) adore her!
Who am mad to lay my spirit prostrate palpably before
 her —
I may enter at her portal soon, as now her lattice
 takes me,
And by noontide as by midnight make her mine, as
 hers she makes me!

ROBERT BROWNING.

SONNET FROM PETRARCH.

GENTLE severity, repulses mild,
 Full of chaste love and pity sorrowing;
 Graceful rebukes, that had the power to bring
 Back to itself a heart by dreams beguiled;
A tender voice, whose accents undefiled
 Held sweet restraints, all duty honoring;
 The bloom of virtue; purity's sweet spring
 To cleanse away base thoughts and passions wild;

Divinest eyes to make a lover's bliss,
　　Whether to bridle in the wayward mind
　　Lest its wild wanderings should the pathway miss,
Or else its griefs to soothe, its wounds to bind, —
　　This sweet completeness of thy life it is
　　Which saved my soul; no other peace I find.

　　　　　　　THOMAS WENTWORTH HIGGINSON

AMY WENTWORTH.

HER fingers shame the ivory keys
　　They dance so light along;
The bloom upon her parted lips
　　Is sweeter than the song.

O perfumed suitor, spare thy smiles!
　　Her thoughts are not of thee;
She better loves the salted wind,
　　The voices of the sea.

Her heart is like an outbound ship
　　That at its anchor swings;
The murmur of the stranded shell
　　Is in the song she sings.

She sings, and, smiling, hears her praise,
　　But dreams the while of one
Who watches from his sea-blown deck
　　The icebergs in the sun.

She questions all the winds that blow,
   And every fog-wreath dim,
And bids the sea-birds flying north
   Bear messages to him.

She speeds them with the thanks of men
   He perilled life to save,
And grateful prayers like holy oil
   To smooth for him the wave.

Brown Viking of the fishing-smack !
   Fair toast of all the town !
The skipper's jerkin ill beseems
   The lady's silken gown !

But ne'er shall Amy Wentworth wear
   For him the blush of shame
Who dares to set his manly gifts
   Against her ancient name.

The stream is brightest at its spring,
   And blood is not like wine ;
Nor honored less than he who heirs
   Is he who founds a line.

Full lightly shall the prize be won,
   If love be Fortune's spur ;
And never maiden stoops to him
   Who lifts himself to her.

Her home is brave in Jaffrey Street,
  With stately stairways worn
By feet of old Colonial knights
  And ladies gentle born.

Still green about its ample porch
  The English ivy twines,
Trained back to show in English oak
  The herald's carven signs.

And on her, from the wainscot old,
  Ancestral faces frown, —
And this has worn the soldier's sword,
  And that the judge's gown.

But, strong of will and proud as they.
  She walks the gallery floor
As if she trod her sailor's deck
  By stormy Labrador !

The sweetbrier blooms on Kittery side,
  And green are Elliot's bowers ;
Her garden is the pebbled beach,
  The mosses are her flowers.

She looks across the harbor-bar
  To see the white gulls fly ;
His greeting from the Northern sea
  Is in their clanging cry.

She hums a song, and dreams that he,
    As in its romance old,
Shall homeward ride with silken sails
    And masts of beaten gold !

O, rank is good, and gold is fair,
    And high and low mate ill ;
But love has never known a law
    Beyond its own sweet will !

JOHN GREENLEAF WHITTIER.

UN BACIO DATO NON È MAI PERDUTO

BECAUSE we once drove together
        In the moonlight over the snow,
With the sharp bells ringing their tinkling chime,
    So many a year ago,

So, now, as I hear them jingle,
    The winter comes back again,
Though the summer stirs in the heavy trees,
    And the wild rose scents the lane.

We gather our furs around us,
    Our faces the keen air stings,
And noiseless we fly o'er the snow-hushed world
    Almost as if we had wings.

Enough is the joy of mere living,
  Enough is the blood's quick thrill;
We are simply happy, I care not why,
  We are happy beyond our will

The trees are with icicles jewelled,
  The walls are o'er-surfed with snow;
The houses with marble-whiteness are roofed,
  In their windows the home-lights glow.

Through the tense, clear sky above us
  The keen stars flash and gleam,
And wrapped in their silent shroud of snow
  The broad fields lie and dream.

And jingling with low, sweet clashing
  Ring the bells as our good horse goes,
And tossing his head, from his nostrils' red
  His frosty breath he blows.

And closely you nestle against me,
  While around your waist my arm
I have slipped — 't is so bitter, bitter cold —
  It is only to keep us warm.

We talk, and then we are silent;
  And suddenly — you know why —
I stooped — could I help it? You lifted your face —
  We kissed — there was nobody nigh.

I never told it — did you, dear ? —
　From that day unto this ;
But my memory keeps in its inmost recess,
　Like a perfume, that innocent kiss.

I dare say you have forgotten,
　'T was so many a year ago,
Or you may not choose to remember it,
　Time may have changed you so.

The world so chills us and kills us,
　Perhaps you may scorn to recall
That night, with its innocent impulse,
　Perhaps you 'll deny it all.

But if, of that fresh sweet nature
　The veriest vestige survive,
You remember that moment's madness, —
　You remember that moonlight drive.

　　　　　　WILLIAM WETMORE STORY.

THE DOORSTEP.

THE conference-meeting through at last,
　　We boys around the vestry waited
To see the girls come tripping past,
　Like snow-birds willing to be mated.

Not braver he that leaps the wall
　By level musket-flashes litten,
Than I, that stepped before them all
　Who longed to see me get the mitten.

But no, she blushed and took my arm!
  We let the old folks have the highway,
And started toward the Maple Farm
  Along a kind of lover's by-way.

I can't remember what we said,
  'T was nothing worth a song or story;
Yet that rude path by which we sped
  Seemed all transformed and in a glory.

The snow was crisp beneath our feet,
  The moon was full, the fields were gleaming;
By hood and tippet sheltered sweet,
  Her face with youth and health was beaming.

The little hand outside her muff, —
  O sculptor, if you could but mould it! —
So lightly touched my jacket cuff,
  To keep it warm I had to hold it.

To have her with me there alone, —
  'T was love and fear and triumph blended.
At last we reached the worn foot-stone
  Where that delicious journey ended.

The old folks too were almost home;
  Her dimpled hand the latches fingered.
We heard the voices nearer come,
  Yet on the doorstep still we lingered.

6

She shook her ringlets from her hood,
    And with a " Thank you, Ned," dissembled;
But yet I knew she understood
    With what a daring wish I trembled.

A cloud passed kindly overhead,
    The moon was slyly peeping through it,
Yet hid its face, as if it said,
    " Come, now or never! do it! *do it!* "

My lips till then had only known
    The kiss of mother and of sister ;
But somehow, full upon her own
    Sweet, rosy, darling mouth — I kissed her!

Perhaps 't was boyish love; yet still,
    O listless woman, weary lover!
To feel once more that fresh, wild thrill
    I 'd give — but who can live youth over ?

                    EDMUND CLARENCE STEDMAN.

BEFORE THE GATE.

THEY gave the whole long day to idle laughter,
    To fitful song and jest,
To moods of soberness as idle, after,
    And silences, as idle too as the rest.

But when at last, upon their way returning,
    Taciturn, late, and loath,
Through the broad meadow in the sunset burning,
    They reached the gate, one fine spell hindered
      them both.

Her heart was troubled with a subtile anguish
    Such as but women know
That wait, and lest love speak or speak not languish,
    And what they would, would rather they would
      not so.

Till he said, — man-like, nothing comprehending
    Of all the wondrous guile
That women won win themselves with, and bending
    Eyes of relentless asking on her the while, —

" Ah, if beyond this gate the path united
    Our steps as far as death,
And I might open it ! — " His voice, affrighted
    At its own daring, faltered under his breath.

Then she — whom both his faith and fear enchanted
    Far beyond words to tell,
Feeling her woman's finest wit had wanted
    The art he had that knew to blunder so well —

Shyly drew near a little step, and mocking,
    " Shall we not be too late
For tea? " she said. " I 'm quite worn out with walking.
    Yes, thanks, your arm. And will you — open the
      gate ? "
                    WILLIAM D. HOWELLS.

IN LOVE'S OWN TIME.

HAD I but earlier known that from the eyes
　　Of that bright soul that fires me like the sun,
　I might have drawn new strength my race to run,
　Burning as burns the phœnix ere it dies ;
Even as the stag or lynx or leopard flies
　　To seek his pleasure and his pain to shun,
　Each word, each smile of her would I have won,
　Flying where now sad age all flight denies.
Yet why complain ?　For even now I find
　In that glad angel's face, so full of rest,
　Health, and content, heart's ease and peace of mind.
Perchance I might have been less simply blest,
　Finding her sooner : if 't is age alone
　That lets me soar with her to seek God's throne.

MICHAEL ANGELO.

GARDEN-FANCIES.

THE FLOWER'S NAME.

HERE 'S the garden she walked across,
　　Arm in my arm, such a short while since :
Hark, now I push its wicket, the moss
　Hinders the hinges and makes them wince !
She must have reached this shrub ere she turned,
　As back with that murmur the wicket swung ;
For she laid the poor snail, my chance foot spurned,
　To feed and forget it the leaves among.

Down this side of the gravel-walk
    She went while her robe's edge brushed the box:
And here she paused in her gracious talk
    To point me a moth on the milk-white flox.
Roses, ranged in valiant row,
    I will never think that she passed you by!
She loves you, noble roses, I know;
    But yonder see, where the rock-plants lie!

This flower she stopped at, finger on lip,
    Stooped over, in doubt, as settling its claim;
Till she gave me, with pride to make no slip,
    Its soft meandering Spanish name.
What a name! was it love, or praise?
    Speech half-asleep, or song half-awake?
I must learn Spanish, one of these days,
    Only for that slow sweet name's sake.

Roses, if I live and do well,
    I may bring her, one of these days,
To fix you fast with as fine a spell,
    Fit you each with his Spanish phrase!
But do not detain me now; for she lingers
    There, like sunshine over the ground,
And ever I see her soft white fingers
    Searching after the bud she found.

Flower, you Spaniard, look that you grow not,
    Stay as you are and be loved forever!
Bud, if I kiss you 't is that you blow not,
    Mind, the shut pink mouth opens never!

For while thus it pouts, her fingers wrestle,
  Twinkling the audacious leaves between,
Till round they turn and down they nestle —
  Is not the dear mark still to be seen?

Where I find her not, beauties vanish;
  Whither I follow her, beauties flee;
Is there no method to tell her in Spanish
  June 's twice June since she breathed it with me?
Come, bud, show me the least of her traces,
  Treasure my lady's lightest footfall —
Ah, you may flout and turn up your faces —
  Roses, you are not so fair after all.

ROBERT BROWNING.

TRUE LOVE.

LET me not to the marriage of true minds
    Admit impediments.   Love is not love
Which alters when it alteration finds,
Or bends with the remover to remove:
O, no! it is an ever-fixed mark
That looks on tempests and is never shaken;
It is the star to every wandering bark,
Whose worth 's unknown, although his height be taken
Love 's not Time's fool, though rosy lips and cheeks
Within his bending sickle's compass come;
Love alters not with his brief hours and weeks,
But bears it out even to the edge of doom.
If this be error and upon me proved,
I never writ, nor no man ever loved.

WILLIAM SHAKSPERE.

THE BROOK-SIDE.

I WANDERED by the brook-side,
  I wandered by the mill ;
I could not hear the brook flow —
  The noisy wheel was still.
There was no burr of grasshopper,
  No chirp of any bird,
But the beating of my own heart
  Was all the sound I heard.

I sat beneath the elm-tree :
  I watched the long, long shade,
And, as it grew still longer,
  I did not feel afraid ;
For I listened for a footfall,
  I listened for a word —
But the beating of my own heart
  Was all the sound I heard.

He came not, — no, he came not —
  The night came on alone —
The little stars sat one by one,
  Each on his golden throne ;
The evening wind passed by my cheek,
  The leaves above were stirred —
But the beating of my own heart
  Was all the sound I heard.

Fast silent tears were flowing,
  When something stood behind;
A hand was on my shoulder —
  I knew its touch was kind;
It drew me nearer — nearer —
  We did not speak one word,
For the beating of our own hearts
  Was all the sound we heard.

RICHARD MONCKTON MILNES.

LOVE'S JUSTIFICATION.

IT must be right sometimes to entertain
  Chaste love with hope not over-credulous:
Since if all human loves were impious,
Unto what end did God the world ordain?
If I love thee and bend beneath thy reign,
  'T is for the sake of beauty glorious
  Which in thine eyes divine is stored for us,
And drives all evil thought from its domain.
That is not love whose tyranny we own
  In loveliness that every moment dies;
  Which, like the face it worships, fades away:
True love is that which the pure heart hath known,
  Which alters not with time or death's decay,
  Yielding on earth earnest of Paradise.

MICHAEL ANGELO.

A FOREBODING.

WHAT were the whole void world, if thou wert
       dead,
Whose briefest absence can eclipse my day,
And make the hours that danced with Time away
Drag their funereal steps with muffled tread?
Through thee, meseems, the very rose is red,
From thee draw life all things that grow not gray,
And by thy force the happy stars are sped.
Thou near, the hope of thee to overflow
Fills all my earth and heaven, and when in Spring,
Ere April come, the birds and blossoms know,
And grasses brighten round her feet to cling;
Nay, and this hope delights all nature so
That the dumb turf I tread on seems to sing.

                  JAMES RUSSELL LOWELL.

THE LOVER'S NIGHT THOUGHTS.

WEARY with toil, I haste me to my bed,
      The dear repose for limbs with travel tired;
But then begins a journey in my head,
To work my mind, when body's work's expired:
For then my thoughts, from far where I abide,
Intend a zealous pilgrimage to thee,
And keep my drooping eyelids open wide,
Looking on darkness which the blind do see:
Save that my soul's imaginary sight
Presents thy shadow to my sightless view,

Which, like a jewel hung in ghastly night,
Makes black night beauteous and her old face new.
Lo ! thus, by day my limbs, by night my mind,
For thee and for myself no quiet find.

WILLIAM SHAKSPERE

NIGHT THOUGHTS.

'TIS sweeter than all else below,
    The daylight and its duties done,
To fold the arms for rest, and so
    Relinquish all regards but one;
To see her features in the dark;
    To lie and meditate once more,
Some grace he did not fully mark,
    Some tone he had not heard before;
Then from beneath his head to take
    Her notes, her picture, and her glove,
Put there for joy when he shall wake,
    And press them to the heart of love;
And then to whisper " Wife," and pray
    To live so long as not to miss
That unimaginable day
    Which farther seems the nearer 't is;
And still from joy's unfathomed well
    To drink, in sleep, while, on her brow
Of innocence ineffable,
    The laughing bridal roses blow.

COVENTRY PATMORE.

WITH A HAND-GLASS.

A PICTURE-FRAME for you to fill,
 A paltry setting for your face,
A thing that has no worth until
 You lend it something of your grace,

I send (unhappy I that sing
 Laid by awhile upon the shelf)
Because I would not send a thing
 Less charming than you are yourself.

And happier than I, alas!
 (Dumb thing, I envy its delight)
'T will wish you well, the looking-glass,
 And look you in the face to-night.

ROBERT LOUIS STEVENSON.

TO LUCASTA.

TELL me not, sweet, I am unkind,
 That from the nunnery
Of thy chaste breast and quiet mind,
 To war and arms I fly.

True, a new mistress now I chase,
 The first foe in the field;
And with a stronger faith embrace
 A sword, a horse, a shield.

Yet this inconstancy is such
    As you too shall adore;
I could not love thee, dear, so much,
    Loved I not honor more.

RICHARD LOVELACE.

TELEPATHY.

" AND how could you dream of meeting?"
    Nay, how can you ask me, sweet?
All day my pulse had been beating
    The tune of your coming feet.

And as nearer and ever nearer
    I felt the throb of your tread,
To be in the world grew dearer,
    And my blood ran rosier red.

Love called, and I could not linger,
    But sought the forbidden tryst,
As music follows the finger
    Of the dreaming lutanist.

And though you had said it and said it,
    "We must not be happy to-day,"
Was I not wiser to credit
    The fire in my feet than your nay?

JAMES RUSSELL LOWELL.

MY LOVE.

IF on the clustering curls of thy dark hair,
 And the pure arching of thy polished brow,
We only gaze, we fondly dream that thou
Art one of those bright ministers who bear,
Along the cloudless bosom of the air,
 Sweet solemn words, to which our spirits bow, —
 With such a holy smile thou lookest now,
And art so soft and delicately fair.

A veil of tender light is mantling o'er thee;
 Around thy opening lips young loves are playing,
 And crowds of youths, in passionate thought de-
 laying,
Pause, as thou movest by them, to adore thee;
 By many a sudden blush and tear betraying
How the heart trembles when it bends before thee!

JAMES GATES PERCIVAL.

"I 'LL NEVER LOVE THEE MORE."

MY dear and only love, I pray
 That little world of thee
Be governed by no other sway
 But purest monarchy:
For if confusion have a part,
 Which virtuous souls abhor,
And hold a synod in thy heart,
 I 'll never love thee more.

As Alexander I will reign,
   And I will reign alone :
My thoughts did evermore disdain
   A rival on my throne.
He either fears his fate too much,
   Or his deserts are small,
Who dares not to put it to the touch
   To gain or lose it all.

But, if no faithless action stain
   Thy love and constant word,
I 'll make thee famous by my pen,
   And glorious by my sword.
I 'll serve thee in such noble ways
   As ne'er were known before ;
I 'll deck and crown thy head with bays,
   And love thee more and more.

                    MARQUIS OF MONTROSE.

LOVE CEREMONIOUS.

KEEP your undrest, familiar style
      For strangers, but respect your friend,
Her most, whose matrimonial smile
   Is, and asks honor without end.
'T is found, and needs it must so be,
   That life from love's allegiance flags,
When love forgets his majesty
   In sloth's unceremonious rags.

Love should make home a stately Court :
   There let the world's rude, hasty ways
Be fashioned to a loftier port,
   And learn to bow and stand at gaze ;
And let the sweet, respective sphere
   Of personal worship there obtain
Circumference for moving clear,
   None treading on another's train.
This makes that pleasures do not cloy,
   And dignifies our mortal strife
With calmness and considerate joy
   Befitting our immortal life.

COVENTRY PATMORE.

O FILIA PULCHRA!

HOW your sweet face revives again
   The dear old time, my Pearl, —
If I may use the pretty name
   I called you when a girl.

You are so young; while Time of me
   Has made a cruel prey,
It has forgotten you, nor swept
   One grace of youth away.

The same sweet face, the same sweet smile,
   The same lithe figure, too ! —
What did you say ?   It was perchance
   Your mother that I knew ?

Ah, yes, of course, it must have been,
 And yet the same you seem,
And for a moment, all these years
 Fled from me like a dream.

Then what your mother would not give,
 Permit me, dear, to take,
The old man's privilege — a kiss —
 Just for your mother's sake.

      WILLIAM WETMORE STORY.

UPON JULIA'S CLOTHES.

WHENAS in silk my Julia goes,
 Then, then, methinks, how sweetly flows
That liquefaction of her clothes.
Next, when I cast mine eyes, and see
That brave vibration each way free :
Oh, how that glittering taketh me !

      ROBERT HERRICK.

THE LETTERS.

STILL on the tower stood the vane,
 A black yew gloom'd the stagnant air,
I peer'd athwart the chancel pane
 And saw the altar cold and bare.
A clog of lead was round my feet,
 A band of pain across my brow;
" Cold altar, Heaven and earth shall meet
 Before you hear my marriage vow."

I turn'd and humm'd a bitter song
　　That mock'd the wholesome human heart,
And then we met in wrath and wrong,
　　We met, but only meant to part.
Full cold my greeting was and dry ;
　　She faintly smiled, she hardly moved ;
I saw with half-unconscious eye
　　She wore the colors I approved.

She took the little ivory chest,
　　With half a sigh she turn'd the key,
Then raised her head with lips comprest,
　　And gave my letters back to me.
And gave the trinkets and the rings,
　　My gifts, when gifts of mine could please :
As looks a father on the things
　　Of his dead son, I look'd on these.

She told me all her friends had said ;
　　I raged against the public liar ;
She talk'd as if her love were dead,
　　But in my words were seeds of fire.
" No more of love ; your sex is known :
　　I never will be twice deceived.
Henceforth I trust the man alone,
　　The woman cannot be believed.

" Thro' slander, meanest spawn of Hell
　　(And woman's slander is the worst),
And you, whom once I loved so well,
　　Thro' you, my life will be accurst."

7

I spoke with heart, and heat and force,
    I shook her breast with vague alarms —
Like torrents from a mountain source
    We rushed into each other's arms.

We parted : sweetly gleam'd the stars,
    And sweet the vapor-braided blue ;
Low breezes fann'd the belfry bars,
    As homeward by the church I drew.
The very graves appear'd to smile,
    So fresh they rose in shadow'd swells ;
"Dark porch," I said, "and silent aisle,
    There comes a sound of marriage bells."

ALFRED TENNYSON.

JENNY KISSED ME.

JENNY kissed me when we met,
    Jumping from the chair she sat in ;
Time, you thief! who love to get
    Sweets into your list, put that in.
Say I 'm weary, say I 'm sad ;
    Say that health and wealth have missed me ;
Say I 'm growing old, but add —
            Jenny kissed me!

LEIGH HUNT.

SINCE THERE'S NO HELP.

SINCE there's no help, come, let us kiss and part!
  Nay, I have done; you get no more of me;
And I am glad, yea, glad with all my heart,
That thus so clearly I myself can free.
Shake hands forever, cancel all our vows,
And when we meet at any time again,
Be it not seen, on either of our brows,
That we one jot of former love retain.

Now at the last gasp of love's latest breath,
When, his pulse failing, passion speechless lies,
When faith is kneeling by his bed of death,
And innocence is closing up his eyes;
Now, if thou wouldst, when all have given him over,
From death to life thou might'st him yet recover.

MICHAEL DRAYTON.

NO TIME TO HATE.

I HAD no time to hate, because
  The grave would hinder me,
And life was not so ample I
Could finish enmity.

Nor had I time to love; but since
Some industry must be,
The little toil of love, I thought,
Was large enough for me.

EMILY DICKINSON.

A WOMAN'S ANSWER.

I WILL not let you say a woman's part
      Must be to give exclusive love alone;
Dearest, although I love you so, my heart
      Answers a thousand claims besides your own.

I love, — what do I not love?   Earth and air
      Find space within my heart, and myriad things
You would not deign to heed are cherished there,
      And vibrate on its very inmost strings.

I love the summer, with her ebb and flow
      Of light and warmth and music, that have nursed
Her tender buds to blossoms ; . . . and you know
      It was in summer that I saw you first.

I love the winter dearly too, . . . but then
      I owe it so much ; on a winter's day,
Bleak, cold and stormy, you returned again,
      When you had been those weary months away.

I love the stars like friends; so many nights
      I gazed at them, when you were far from me,
Till I grew blind with tears; . . . those far-off lights
      Could watch you, whom I longed in vain to see.

I love the flowers; happy hours lie
   Shut up within their petals close and fast:
You have forgotten, dear; but they and I
   Keep every fragment of the golden Past.

I love, too, to be loved; all loving praise
   Seems like a crown upon my life, — to make
It better worth the giving, and to raise
   Still nearer to your own the heart you take.

I love all good and noble souls; — I heard
   One speak of you but lately, and for days,
Only to think of it, my soul was stirrred
   In tender memory of such generous praise.

I love all those who love you, all who owe
   Comfort to you; and I can find regret
Even for those poorer hearts who once could know,
   And once could love you, and can now forget.

Well, is my heart so narrow, — I, who spare
   Love for all these? Do I not even hold
My favorite books in special tender care,
   And prize them as a miser does his gold?

The poets that you used to read to me
   While summer twilights faded in the sky;
But most of all I think Aurora Leigh
   Because — because — do you remember why?

Will you be jealous?   Did you guess before
  I loved so many things? — Still you the best; —
Dearest, remember that I love you more,
  O more a thousand times, than all the rest!

ADELAIDE A. PROCTER.

A REMINISCENCE.

'TWAS April; 't was Sunday; the day was fair, —
    Yes! sunny and fair.
    And how happy was I!
You wore the white dress you loved to wear;
And two little flowers were hid in your hair —
    Yes! in your hair —
    On that day — gone by!

We sat on the moss; it was shady and dry, —
    Yes! shady and dry;
    And we sat in the shadow.
We looked at the leaves, we looked at the sky,
We looked at the brook which bubbled near by, —
    Yes, bubbled near by,
    Through the quiet meadow.

A bird sang on the swinging vine, —
    Yes, on the vine, —
    And then, — sang not;
I took your little white hand in mine;
'T was April; 't was Sunday; 't was warm sunshine, —
    Yes, warm sunshine:
    Have you forgot?

Translation: JAMES FREEMAN CLARKE.

LOVE FOR LOVE'S SAKE.

IF thou must love me, let it be for nought
    Except for love's sake only. Do not say
" I love her for her smile, . . her look, . . her way
Of speaking gently, . . for a trick of thought
That falls in well with mine, and certes brought
A sense of pleasant ease on such a day " —
For these things in themselves, Beloved, may
Be changed or change for thee, — and love so wrought
May be unwrought so. Neither love me for
Thine own dear pity's wiping my cheeks dry:
A creature might forget to weep, who bore
Thy comfort long, and lose thy love thereby.
But love me for love's sake, that evermore
Thou mays't love on through love's eternity.

              ELIZABETH BARRETT BROWNING.

"WHEN YOU ARE OLD."

WHEN you are old, and I am passed away —
    Passed, and your face, your golden face is
       gray —
I think whate'er the end, this dream of mine,
Comforting you, a friendly star will shine
Down the dim slope where still you stumble and stray.

So may it be : that no dead Yesterday,
No sad-eyed ghost, but generous and gay,
May serve you memories like almighty wine,
            When you are old.

Dear Heart, it shall be so. Under the sway
Of death the past's enormous disarray
Lies hushed and dark. Yet though there come no
    sign,
Live on well pleased : immortal and divine,
Love shall still tend you, as God's angels may,
                When you are old.

WILLIAM ERNEST HENLEY.

IDEAL LOVE.

HE who loves truly, grows in force and might;
    For beauty and the image of his love
    Expand his spirit : whence he burns to prove
    Adventures high, and hold all perils light.
If thus a lady's love dilate the knight,
    What glories and what joy all joys above
    Shall not the heavenly splendor, joined by love
    Unto our flesh-imprisoned soul, excite?
Once freed, she would become one sphere immense
    Of love, power, wisdom, filled with Deity,
    Elate with wonders of the eternal Sense.
But we like sheep and wolves war ceaselessly:
    That love we never seek, that light intense,
    Which would exalt us to infinity.

MICHAEL ANGELO.

FIRST WORDS OF LOVE.
From painting by C. E. Perugini.

LETTICE.

I SAID to Lettice, our sister Lettice,
  While drooped and glistened her eyelash brown,
"Your man's a poor man, a cold and dour man,
  There's many a better about our town."
She smiled securely — "He loves me purely:
  A true heart's safe, both in smile or frown;
And nothing harms me while his love warms me,
  Whether the world go up or down."

"He comes of strangers, and they are rangers,
  And ill to trust, girl, when out of sight:
Fremd folk may blame ye, and e'en defame ye, —
  A gown oft handled looks seldom white."
She raised serenely her eyelids queenly, —
  "My innocence is my whitest gown;
No harsh tongue grieves me while he believes me,
  Whether the world go up or down."

"Your man's a frail man, was ne'er a hale man,
  And sickness knocketh at every door,
And death comes making bold hearts cower, break-
    ing — "
  Our Lettice trembled, — but once, no more.
"If death should enter, smite to the centre
  Our poor home palace, all crumbling down,
He cannot fright us, nor disunite us,
  Life bears Love's cross, death brings Love's crown."

                    DINAH MULOCK CRAIK.

TO E. B. B.

GOD be thanked, the meanest of his creatures
    Boasts two soul-sides, one to face the world with,
One to show a woman when he loves her.

This I say of me, but think of you, Love!
This to you — yourself my moon of poets!
Ah, but that 's the world's side, — there 's the wonder, —
Thus they see you, praise you, think they know you.
There, in turn I stand with them and praise you,
Out of my own self, I dare to phrase it.
But the best is when I glide from out them,
Cross a step or two of dubious twilight,
Come out on the other side, the novel
Silent silver lights and darks undreamed of,
Where I hush and bless myself with silence.

Oh, their Rafael of the dear Madonnas,
Oh, their Dante of the dread Inferno,
Wrote one song, — and in my brain I sing it;
Drew one angel, — borne, see, on my bosom!

                              ROBERT BROWNING.

AT LAST.

IN the day the sun is darkened,
    And the moon as blood,
And the earth is swept to ruin
    On the avenging flood,

Come to me — Then give thyself
To my arms and kiss;
We shall not know that all is lost,
So great shall be our bliss.

STOPFORD BROOKE.

SONG.

IN Love, if Love be Love, if Love be ours,
Faith and unfaith can ne'er be equal powers:
Unfaith in aught is want of faith in all.

It is the little rift within the lute
That by and by will make the music mute,
And ever widening slowly silence all.

The little rift within the lover's lute,
Or little pitted speck in garnered fruit
That, rotting inward, slowly moulders all.

It is not worth the keeping, — let it go:
But shall it? Answer, darling; answer, No.
And trust me not at all, or all in all.

ALFRED TENNYSON.

THE COURSE OF LOVE.

HER father loved me; oft invited me;
Still questioned me the story of my life,
From year to year, the battles, sieges, fortunes,
That I have passed.

I ran it through, even from my boyish days,
To the very moment that he bade me tell it. . . .

                These things to hear
Would Desdemona seriously incline :
But still the house-affairs would draw her thence :
Which ever as she could with haste despatch,
She 'ld come again, and with a greedy ear
Devour up my discourse : which I observing,
Took once a pliant hour, and found good means
To draw from her a prayer of earnest heart
That I would all my pilgrimage dilate,
Whereof by parcels she had something heard,
But not intentively : I did consent,
And often did beguile her of her tears,
When I did speak of some distressful stroke
That my youth suffered.   My story being done,
She gave me for my pains a world of sighs :
She swore, in faith, 't was strange, 't was passing
    strange,
'T was pitiful, 't was wondrous pitiful :
She wished she had not heard it ; yet she wished
That heaven had made her such a man : she thanked
    me,
And bade me, if I had a friend that loved her,
I should but teach him how to tell my story,
And that would woo her.   Upon this hint I spake :
She loved me for the dangers I had passed,
And I loved her that she did pity them.
This only is the witchcraft I have used :
Here comes the lady ; let her witness it.

                    WILLIAM SHAKSPERE.

SOME DAY OF DAYS.

SOME day, some day of days, threading the street
      With idle, heedless pace,
      Unlooking for such grace,
      I shall behold your face !
Some day, some day of days, thus may we meet.

Perchance the sun may shine from skies of May,
      Or winter's icy chill
      Touch whitely vale and hill.
      What matter ?   I shall thrill
Through every vein with summer on that day.

Once more life's perfect youth will all come back,
      And for a moment there
      I shall stand fresh and fair,
      And drop the garment care,
Once more my perfect youth will nothing lack.

I shut my eyes now, thinking how 't will be, —
      How face to face each soul
      Will slip its long control,
      Forget the dismal dole
Of dreary Fate's dark separating sea ;

And glance to glance and hand to hand in greeting,
      The past with all its fears,
      Its silence and its tears,
      Its lonely yearning years,
Shall vanish in the moment of that meeting.

                                        NORA PERRY.

THE PARADOX.

HOW strange a thing a Lover seems
        To animals that do not love!
Look where he walks and talks in dreams,
        And flouts us with his Lady's glove!
How foreign is the garb he wears,
        And how his great devotion mocks
Our poor propriety, and scares
        The undevout with paradox!
His soul, through scorn of worldly care,
        And great extremes of sweet and gall,
And musing much on all that 's fair,
        Grows witty and fantastical;
He sobs his joy and sings his grief,
        And evermore finds such delight
In simply picturing his relief,
        That 'plaining seems to cure his plight.
He makes his sorrow when there 's none;
        His fancy blows both cold and hot;
Next to the wish that she 'll be won,
        His first hope is that she may not.
He sues, yet deprecates consent;
        Would she be captured, she must fly;
She looks too happy and content,
        For whose least pleasure he would die.
Oh, cruelty, she cannot care
        For one to whom she 's always kind!
He says he 's naught, but oh, despair,
        If he 's not Jove to her fond mind!

He's jealous if she pets a dove,
   She must be his with all her soul;
Yet 't is a postulate in love
   That part is greater than the whole,
And all his apprehension's stress,
   When he's with her, regards her hair,
Her hand, a ribbon of her dress, —
   As if his life were only there.
Because she's constant, he will change,
   And kindest glances coldly meet;
And all the time he seems so strange,
   His soul is fawning at her feet.
Of smiles and simple heaven grown tired,
   He wickedly provokes her tears;
And when she weeps, as he desired,
   Falls slain with ecstasies of fears;
He finds, although she has no fault,
   Except the folly to be his;
He worships her the more to exalt
   The profanation of a kiss.
Health's his disease; he's never well
   But when his paleness shames her rose;
His faith's a rock-built citadel,
   Its sign a flag that each way blows;
His o'erfed fancy frets and fumes,
   And Love in him is fierce like Hate,
And ruffles his ambrosial plumes
   Against the bars of time and fate.

COVENTRY PATMORE.

PARTED.

DO not write. I am sad, and would my life were
o'er.
  A summer without thee? Oh, night of starless
    gloom !
I fold the idle arms that cannot clasp thee more;
  To knock at my heart's door were like knocking on
    a tomb.
        Do not write.

Do not write. We will learn unto ourselves to die.
  Ask God, or ask thyself of my love, if thou wouldst
    know;
But to hear thee calling far away and calling tenderly,
  Were to hear the songs of Heaven afar and never
    hope to go.
        Do not write.

Do not write; for I fear thee. I do not dare to think
  How thy voice was wont to sound, lest it seem to
    call anew.
Do not show living water to one who cannot drink ;
  The writing of a friend is a likeness passing true.
        Do not write.

Do not write those sweet words, for I may not read
    them now ;
They would flood my foolish heart with a deceitful
    bliss.

They are brilliant with thy smile, with thy tenderness
    aglow;
I could not choose but dream thou hadst sealed
    them with a kiss.
        Do not write.

                MADAME DESBORDES-VALMORE.

SPECULATIVE.

OTHERS may need new life in Heaven;
    Man, Nature, Art made new, assume!
Man with new mind old sense to leaven,
    Nature — new light to clear old gloom,
Art that breaks bounds, gets soaring room.

I shall pray: " Fugitive as precious —
    Minutes which passed, — return, remain!
Let earth's old life once more enmesh us,
    You with old pleasure, me — old pain,
So we but meet nor part again! "

                ROBERT BROWNING.

HER HELPFULNESS.

YEA, let me praise my lady whom I love,
    Likening her unto the lily and rose:
    Brighter than morning star her visage glows;
She is beneath even as her Saint above:
She is as the air in summer which God wove

8

Of purple and vermilion glorious ;
  As gold and jewels richer than man knows.
Love's self, being love for her, must holier prove.
Ever as she walks she hath a sober grace,
    Making bold men abashed and good men glad ;
      If she delight thee not, thy heart must err.
No man dare look on her, his thoughts being base ;
    Nay, let me say even more than I have said :
      No man could think base thoughts who looked
        on her.

                    DANTE : *Vita Nuova.*

THE FIRST LESSON.

NOT in this world to see his face
    Sounds long, until I read the place
Where this is said to be
But just the primer to a life
Unopened, rare, upon the shelf
Clasped yet to him and me.

And yet, my primer suits me so
I would not choose a book to know
Than that, be sweeter wise ;
Might some one else so learned be,
And leave me just my A B C,
Himself could have the skies.

                    EMILY DICKINSON.

WHO KNOW NOT LOVE.

A H ! sad are they who know not love,
But, far from passion's tears and smiles,
Drift down a moonless sea, beyond
The silvery coasts of fairy isles.

And sadder they whose longing lips
Kiss empty air, and never touch
The dear warm mouth of those they love —
Waiting, wasting, suffering much.

But clear as amber, fine as musk
Is life to those who, pilgrim wise,
Move hand in hand from dawn to dusk,
Each morning nearer Paradise.

Oh, not for them shall angels pray !
They stand in everlasting light,
They walk in Allah's smile by day,
And nestle in his heart by night.

THOMAS BAILEY ALDRICH.

THE WEDDING-DAY.

O TRUE and tried, so well and long,
Demand not thou a marriage lay;
In that it is thy marriage day
Is music more than any song.

But where is she, the bridal flower,
  That must be made a wife ere noon?
  She enters, glowing like the moon
Of Eden on its bridal bower:

On me she bends her blissful eyes,
  And then on thee; they meet thy look,
  And brighten like the star that shook
Betwixt the palms of Paradise.

But now set out; the noon is near,
  And I must give away the bride;
  She fears not, or with thee beside
And me behind her, will not fear:

For I that danced her on my knee,
  That watched her on her nurse's arm,
  That shielded a" her life from harm,
At last must part with her to thee;

Now waiting to be made a wife,
  Her feet, my darling, on the dead;
  Their pensive tablets round her head,
And the most living words of life

Breathed in her ear. The ring is on,
  The "wilt thou" answered, and again
  The "wilt thou" asked, till out of twain
Her sweet "I will" has made ye one.

Now sign your names, which shall be read,
  Mute symbols of a joyful morn,
  By village eyes as yet unborn ;
The names are signed, and overhead

Begins the clash and clang that tells
  The joy to every wandering breeze ;
  The blind wall rocks, and on the trees
The dead leaf trembles to the bells.

O happy hour ! and happier hours
  Await them. Many a merry face
  Salutes them, — maidens of the place,
That pelt us in the porch with flowers.

O happy hour ! behold the bride
  With him to whom her hand I gave.
  They leave the porch, they pass the grave
That has to-day its sunny side.

But they must go ; the time draws on,
  And those white-favored horses wait ;
  They rise, but linger, it is late ;
Farewell, we kiss, and they are gone.

A shade falls on us like the dark
  From little cloudlets on the grass,
  But sweeps away as out we pass
To range the woods, to roam the park,

Discussing how their courtship grew,
   And talk of others that are wed,
   And how she looked, and what he said;
And back we come at fall of dew.

Again the feast, the speech, the glee,
   The shade of passing thought, the wealth
   Of words and wit, the double health,
The crowning cup, the three times three,

And last the dance; till I retire:
   Dumb is that tower which spake so loud,
   And high in heaven the streaming cloud,
And on the downs a rising fire:

And rise, O moon, from yonder down,
   Till over down and over dale
   All night the shining vapor sail
And pass the silent-lighted town,

The white-faced halls, the glancing rills,
   And catch at every mountain head,
   And o'er the friths that branch and spread
Their sleeping silver through the hills.

And touch with shade the bridal doors,
   With tender gloom the roof, the wall;
   And breaking let the splendor fall
To spangle all the happy shores
By which they rest.

                Alfred Tennyson.

TO A DAUGHTER ON HER MARRIAGE.

FROM THE FRENCH OF VICTOR HUGO.

BE happy now with him, and love him who loves
   thee;
Adieu! *our* treasure thou hast been, *his* henceforth be.
From home, yet to thy home, O darling child! depart;
Take with thee all the joy — leave us the heavy heart!

We fain would keep thee here, yet there for thee they
     wait;
Wife, daughter, angel, child, — assume thy twofold
     state;
Leave a regret for us, take them a hope the while;
Not without tears go forth, but enter with a smile!

SAMUEL LONGFELLOW.

AN ANGEL IN THE HOUSE.

HOW sweet it were, if without feeble fright,
   Or dying of the dreadful beauteous sight,
An angel came to us, and we could bear
To see him issue from the silent air
At evening in our room, and bend on ours
His divine eyes, and bring us from his bowers
News of dear friends, and children who have never
Been dead indeed — as we shall know forever.

Alas! we think not what we daily see
About our hearths, — angels that *are* to be,
Or may be if they will; and we prepare
Their souls and hours to meet in happy air, —
A child, a friend, a wife, whose soft heart sings
In unison with ours, breeding its future wings.

LEIGH HUNT.

A WEDDING SONG.

JUNE 28, 1865.

TWO roses growing on a single tree,
    Two faces bending o'er a silver spring,
Two pairs of eyes that their own image see,
And set the heavens within a little ring,
Two children in this naughty world of ours,
        Linked by the marriage powers.

Undo the things from off your feet, —
This spot at least is holy ground.
The solitude is wild and sweet,
Where no base thing is found.
There watch, or wander in that Paradise
        Till soft moon-rise.

Sink through the soundless world of dreams,
Or climb the secret stairs of bliss,
And tiptoe stand where brightest gleams
The heaven of heavens within a kiss;

Sleep through the soft hours of rosy morn;
Urania, be born!

Sleep while the moist star trembles in the dews,
And when in sunrise gleams the lake of glass;
Sleep while the heavens are interchanging hues,
And Saturn's tear " rolls down the blade of grass;"
Wake when the birds are singing in the trees,
And sing like these.

JOHN SAVARY.

THE NEWLY WEDDED.

NOW the rite is duly done,
Now the word is spoken,
And the spell has made us one
Which may ne'er be broken:
Rest we, dearest, in our home, —
Roam we o'er the heather, —
We shall rest, and we shall roam,
Shall we not? together.

From this hour the summer rose
Sweeter breathes to charm us;
From this hour the winter snows
Lighter fall to harm us:
Fair or foul — on land or sea —
Come the wind or weather,
Best or worst, whate'er they be,
We shall share together.

Death, who friend from friend can part,
  Brother rend from brother,
Shall but link us, heart and heart,
  Closer to each other :
We will call his anger play,
  Deem his dart a feather,
When we meet him on our way
  Hand in hand together.

WINTHROP MACKWORTH PRAED

A WEDDING SONG.

I SAID : " My heart, now let us sing a song
  For a fair lady on her wedding-day ;
Some solemn hymn or pretty roundelay,
That shall be with her as she goes along
  To meet her joy, and for her happy feet
  Shall make a pleasant music, low and sweet."

Then said my heart : " It is right bold of thee
  To think that any song that we could sing
  Would for this lady be an offering
Meet for such gladness as hers needs must be,
  What time she goes to don her bridal ring,
  And her own heart makes sweetest carolling."

And so it is that with my lute unstrung,
  Lady, I come to greet thy wedding-day ;
But once, methinks, I heard a poet say
The sweetest songs remain for aye unsung.

So mine, unsung, at thy dear feet I lay,
And with a " Peace be with thee ! " go my way.

JOHN W. CHADWICK.

THE DAY-DREAM— THE DEPARTURE.

A ND on her lover's arm she leant,
  And round her waist she felt it fold,
And far across the hills they went
 In that new world which is the old :
Across the hills, and far away
 Beyond their utmost purple rim,
And deep into the dying day
 The happy princess followed him.

" I 'd sleep another hundred years,
 O love, for such another kiss ; "
" Oh, wake forever, love," she hears,
 " O love, 't was such as this and this."
And o 'er them many a sliding star,
 And many a merry wind was borne,
And, streamed through many a golden bar,
 The twilight melted into morn.

" O eyes long laid in happy sleep ! "
 " O happy sleep, that lightly fled ! "
" O happy kiss, that woke thy sleep ! "
 " O love, thy kiss would wake the dead ! "

And o'er them many a flowing range
Of vapor buoyed the crescent bark,
And, rapt through many a rosy change,
The twilight died into the dark.

" A hundred summers ! can it be ?
And whither goest thou, tell me where ? "
" Oh, seek my father's court with me,
For there are greater wonders there."
And o'er the hills, and far away
Beyond their utmost purple rim,
Beyond the night, across the day,
Through all the world she followed him.

ALFRED TENNYSON.

WHEN SHE COMES HOME.

WHEN she comes home again ! A thousand
ways
I fashion, to myself, the tenderness
Of my glad welcome : I shall tremble — yes ;
And touch her as when first in the old days
I touched her girlish hand, nor dared upraise
Mine eyes, such was my faint heart's sweet distress.
Then silence, and the perfume of her dress :
The room will sway a little, and a haze
Cloy eyesight — soul-sight, even — for a space :
And tears, — yes ; and the ache here in the throat,
To know that I so ill deserve the place
Her arms made for me ; and the sobbing note

I stay with kisses, ere the tearful face
Again is hidden in the old embrace.

JAMES WHITCOMB RILEY.

TWO TRUTHS.

" DARLING," he said, "I never meant
To hurt you;" and his eyes were wet.
"I would not hurt you for the world:
Am I to blame if I forget?"

"Forgive my selfish tears!" she cried,
" Forgive! I knew that it was not
Because you meant to hurt me, sweet, —
I knew it was that you forgot."

But all the same, deep in her heart
Rankled this thought, and rankles yet, —
"When love is at its best, one loves
So much that he cannot forget."

H. H. JACKSON

UNKIND WORDS.

IF I had known in the morning
How wearily all the day
The words unkind
Would trouble your mind
That I said when you went away,
I had been more careful, darling,

Nor given you needless pain;
But we vex our own
With look and tone,
We might never take back again.

For though in the quiet evening
You give me a kiss of peace,
Yet it well might be
That never for me
The pain of the heart should cease !
How many go forth in the morning
Who never come home at night !
And hearts have been broken
For harsh words spoken,
That sorrow can ne'er set right.

We have careful thought for the stranger,
And smiles for the sometime guest;
But oft for our own
The bitter tone,
Though we love our own the best.
Ah, lips with the curve impatient !
Ah, brow with the shade of scorn!
'T were a cruel fate
Were the night too late
To undo the work of morn.

ANON.

SUN AND RAIN.

A YOUNG wife stood at the lattice-pane,
  In a study sad and " brown,"
Watching the dreary ceaseless rain
  Steadily pouring down :
      Drip, drip, drip !
  It kept on its tireless play ;
And the poor little woman sighed, " Ah me !
  What a wretched, weary day ! "

An eager hand at the door,
  A step as of one in haste,
A kiss on her lips once more,
  And an arm around her waist :
      Throb, throb, throb !
  Went her little heart grateful and gay,
As she thought, with a smile, " Well after all,
  It is n't so dull a day ! "

Forgot was the plashing rain
  And the lowering skies above,
For the sombre room was lighted again
  By the blessed sun of love :
      " Love, love, love ! "
  Ran the little wife's murmured lay ;
" Without, it may threaten and frown if it will ;
  Within what a golden day ! "

                                        ANON.

HOME SONG.

STAY, stay at home, my heart and rest;
    Home-keeping hearts are happiest,
For those that wander they know not where
Are full of trouble and full of care:
        To stay at home is best.

Weary and homesick and distressed,
They wander east, they wander west,
And are baffled and beaten and blown about
By the winds of the wilderness of doubt:
        To stay at home is best.

Then stay at home, my heart, and rest;
The bird is safest in its nest;
O'er all that flutter their wings and fly
A hawk is hovering in the sky:
        To stay at home is best.

                                        ANON

THE OLDEST STORY.

UNDER the coverlet's snowy fold
    The tiniest stir that ever was seen,
And the tiniest sound, as if fairy folk
Were cuddling under a leaf, I ween.

LOVE AND INNOCENCE.

From painting by L. Perrault.

That is the baby : he came to town
 Only a day or two ago ;
But he looks as wise as if he knew
 All that a baby can ever know.

There he lies in a little heap,
 As soft as velvet, as warm as toast,
As rosy-red as the harvest moon
 Which I saw so big on the hazy coast.

Hear him gurgle and sputter and sigh,
 As if his dear little heart would break,
And scold away as if all the world
 Were only meant for his littleness' sake.

Blink, little eyes, at the strange new light ;
 Hark, little ears, at the strange new sound :
Wonderful things shall you see and hear
 As the days and the months and the years go round.

Hardly you seem a Life at all ;
 Only a Something with hands and feet,
Only a Feeling that things are warm,
 Only a Longing for something to eat.

Have you a thought in your downy head ?
 Can you say to yourself so much as " I " ?
Have you found out yet that you are yourself ?
 Or has God, what you will be by and by ?

9

It's only a little that we can guess,
    But it's quite as much as we care to know,
The rest will come with the fleeting years,
    Little by little, — and better so.

Enough for the day is the good thereof:
    The speck of a thing that is lying there,
And the presence that fills the silent house
    With the tender hush of a voiceless prayer.

                          JOHN W. CHADWICK.

SKETCH OF A YOUNG LADY FIVE MONTHS OLD

MY pretty budding, breathing flower,
        Methinks, if I to-morrow
Could manage, just for half an hour,
        Sir Joshua's brush to borrow,
I might immortalize a few
        Of all the myriad graces
Which Time, while yet they all are new,
        With newer still replaces.

I'd paint, my child, your deep blue eyes,
        Their quick and earnest flashes;
I'd paint the fringe that round them lies,
        The fringe of long dark lashes;
I'd draw with most fastidious care
        One eyebrow, then the other,
And that fair forehead, broad and fair,
        The forehead of your mother.

I 'd oft retouch the dimpled cheek
    Where health in sunshine dances;
And oft the pouting lips, where speak
    A thousand voiceless fancies;
And the soft neck would keep me long, —
    The neck more smooth and snowy
Than ever yet in school-boy's song
    Had Caroline or Chloe.

Not less on those twin rounded arms
    My new-found skill would linger,
Nor less upon the rosy charms
    Of every tiny finger;
Nor slight the small feet, little one,
    So prematurely clever
That, though they neither walk nor run,
    I think they 'd jump forever.

But then your odd endearing ways —
    What study e'er could catch them?
Your aimless gestures, endless plays —
    What canvas e'er could match them?
Your lively leap of merriment,
    Your murmur of petition,
Your serious silence of content,
    Your laugh of recognition.

Here were a puzzling toil, indeed,
    For Art's most fine creations! —
Grow on, sweet baby; we will need,
    To note your transformations,

No picture of your form or face,
　　Your waking or your sleeping,
But that which Love shall daily trace,
　　And trust to Memory's keeping.

Hereafter, when revolving years
　　Have made you tall and twenty,
And brought you blended hopes and fears,
　　And sighs and slaves in plenty,
May those who watch our little saint
　　Among her tasks and duties,
Feel all her virtues hard to paint,
　　As now we deem her beauties.

　　　　　　　　WINTHROP MACKWORTH PRAED.

BABY'S SKIES.

WOULD you know the baby's skies?
　　Baby's skies are mother's eyes.
Mother's eyes and smile together
Make the baby's pleasant weather.

Mother, keep your eyes from tears,
Keep your heart from foolish fears,
Keep your lips from dull complaining,
Lest the baby think 't is raining.

　　　　　　　　MARY C. BARTLETT.

MOTHER.

UPON her snowy couch she drooping lies,
  A languor on her limbs that seems a grace,
A sacred pallor on her lily face,
A blessed light reflected in her eyes, —
She knows who drew her strength, and would not rise;
  Forgetting, she rests a little space,
  Sees her warm life-blood mantle in his face,
And strains her ear to catch his waiting cries.
O wondrous mother-love ! how strange and deep,
  With what vibrating thrill of tenderness;
    To give the glow, and lie a pallid flower,
To give the light, and smile, and wait to weep !
  Sweet is thine infant's warm unconsciousness,
    But sweeter thy mysterious, sacred power !

ELAINE GOODALE.

IN AN UNKNOWN TONGUE.

I KNOW full well what saith Saint Paul, —
  For unknown tongues he did not care;
It was as much as he could do
  To speak them good and fair.

Give him the known and understood;
  Five words of this he counted more
Than thousands ten of all the rest
  That men could babble o'er.

But then he did n't, as he might,
  Like Peter, take a wife about,
To tend his thorn, and soothe his heart,
  With combat wearied out.

And so he had no tiny Paul,
  No nonsense-prating, wee Pauline,
To make him half forget the strife
  His Jew and Greek between.

I cannot glory, as could he,
  In perils both by sea and land;
Of visions I have had a few, —
  Some hard to understand.

But I can glory in a Boy,
  As dear as ever poet sung;
And all his speech, from morn till eve,
  Is in an unknown tongue.

Strange, bubbling, rippling, gurgling sounds
  His pouting lips still overflow;
But what the meaning of them is,
  The wisest do not know.

Friends have I, learned in the Greek,
  In Latin, Hebrew, Spanish, Dutch,
In French and German; and a few
  Of Sanscrit know — not much.

They come and hear the baby's speech,
  As blithe as any song of bird;
They wonder much, but go away,
  Nor understand a word.

It minds me now of mountain rills,
  And now of zigzag droning bees,
And now of sounds the summer makes
  Among the leafy trees.

And yet, if I should say the truth,
  Five words of his to me are more
Than of the words I understand
  Five hundred times a score.

For whatsoever they may mean
  To him or to my learned friends,
One meaning, of all meanings best,
  He still to me commends, —

That life is sweet for him and me,
  Though half its meaning be not guessed;
That God is good, and I a child
  Upon his loving breast.
               JOHN W. CHADWICK.

A RHYME OF ONE.

YOU sleep upon your mother's breast,
    Your race begun,
A welcome, long a wish'd-for Guest,
    Whose age is One.

A Baby-Boy, you wonder why
        You cannot run;
You try to talk — how hard you try!
        You 're only One.

Ere long you won't be such a dunce;
        You 'll eat your bun,
And fly your kite, like folk who once
        Were only One.

You 'll rhyme and woo, and fight and joke,
        Perhaps you 'll pun!
Such feats are never done by folk
        Before they 're One.

Some day, too, you may have your joy,
        And envy none;
Yes, you yourself may own a Boy
        Who is n't One.

He 'll dance and laugh and crow; he 'll do
        As you have done
(You crown a happy home, though you
        Are only One).

But when he 's grown shall you be here
        To share his fun,
And talk of times when he (the Dear!)
        Was hardly One?

LOVE WINS.

From painting by Jean Aubert.

Dear Child, 't is your poor lot to be
  My little Son;
I 'm glad, though I am old, you see, —
  While you are One.

FREDERICK LOCKER.

BABY.

DIMPLED and flushed and dewy pink he lies,
  Crumpled and tossed and lapt in snowy bands;
Aimlessly reaching with his tiny hands,
Lifting in wondering gaze his great blue eyes.
Sweet pouting lips, parted by breathing sighs;
  Soft cheeks, warm tinted as from tropic lands;
  Framed with brown hair in shining silken strands, —
All fair, all pure, a sunbeam from the skies!
  O perfect innocence !   O soul enshrined
    In blissful ignorance of good or ill,
      By never gale of idle passion crossed !
  Although thou art no alien from thy kind,
    Though pain and death may take thee captive, still
      Through sin, at least, thine Eden is not lost.

ELAINE GOODALE.

THE PLAYMATE HOURS.

DAWN lingers silent in the shade of night,
  Till on the gloaming Baby's laughter rings.
  Then smiling Day awakes, and open flings
Her golden doors, to speed the shining flight

Of restless hours, gay children of the light.
   Each eager playfellow to Baby brings
   Some separate gift, — a flitting bird that sings
With her ; a waving branch of berries bright;
A heap of rustling leaves; each trifle cheers
   This joyous little life but just begun.
No weary hour to her brings sighs or tears ;
   And when the shadows warn the loitering sun,
With blossoms in her hands, untouched by fears,
   She softly falls asleep, and day is done.

MRS. T. W. HIGGINSON.

CRADLE SONG.

THE winds are whispering over the sea,
   And the waves are listening smilingly, —
They are telling tales of the shining sky,
And the dusky lands they travel by.

They are telling tales they have often told, —
Of faces new and feelings old,
Of hope and fear, of love and hate,
Of birth and death and human fate,

Of homes of joy and hearts of pain,
Of storm and strife, and peace again,
Of age and youth, of man and maid,
And of baby mine, in the cradle laid.

And the sun laughs down in his own kind way,
For the heart of the sun is as young as they;
And the sea looks up as a loved one should, —
They are old; they know it is good, all good.

You may feel the waves as the cradle swings,
And the air is stirred with the wind's soft wings,
And mother has heard from the sky and sea
That they send " sweet sleep and dreams " to thee.

Then hush ! my baby, gently rest
In the night's wide arms, on the earth's broad breast,
The sky above, beneath the sea,
And a greater than all to shelter thee.

MERLE ST. CROIX WRIGHT.

SOME TIME.

L AST night, my darling, as you slept,
    I thought I heard you sigh,
And to your little crib I crept,
    And watched a space thereby;
And then I stooped and kissed your brow,
    For oh ! I love you so —
You are too young to know it now,
    But some time you shall know !

Some time when, in a darkened place
    Where others come to weep,
Your eyes shall look upon a face
    Calm in eternal sleep.

The voiceless lips, the wrinkled brow,
　The patient smile shall show —
You are too young to know it now,
　But some time you may know !

Look backward, then, into the years,
　And see me here to-night, —
See, O my darling ! how my tears
　Are falling as I write,
And feel once more upon your brow
　The kiss of long ago —
You are too young to know it now,
　But some time you shall know.

　　　　　　　　　　EUGENE FIELD.

WHERE BABY JOY COMES FROM.

AS I sat by my study table,
　With my sermon strewing the floor,
My little sixteen-month darling
　Came full-sail through the study door.
He first bore away to the window,
　Then veered to the bright hearthstone;
But soon in the furthest corner
　Cast anchor all alone.

First he rattled the quills in my pen-box,
　And then with the carpet he played;
Then he washed his hands in the sunshine,
　And caught at the shadows they made.

One thing was as good as another,
  For each gave a new surprise :
And the light of his childish gladness
  Kept shining on out of his eyes.

As I wondered where all the joy came from,
  This thought fell from heaven on me,
That when God and a babe are together,
  A little fountain of glee
Must needs bubble up in the child's heart,
  Because those waters are given,
And ever renewed by the joy tides
  Of the great cheerful Heart in heaven.

I had quite forgotten my sermon,
  And my baby upon the floor
Was tearing the papers to pieces
  That were strewed from window to door ;
But I knew that the thought he gave me
  Was more than his hands could destroy, —
For the love of the Father in heaven
  Had come to me through my boy.

                    SAMUEL R. CALTHROP.

FROM "THE MILLER'S DAUGHTER."

L OOK through mine eyes with thine.   True wife,
    Round my true heart thine arms entwine ;
My other dearer life in life,
  Look through my very soul with thine !

Untouched with any shade of years,
  May those kind eyes forever dwell!
They have not shed a many tears,
  Dear eyes, since first I knew them well.

Yet tears they shed: they had their part
  Of sorrow; for when time was ripe,
The still affection of the heart
  Became an outward breathing type,
That into stillness passed again,
  And left a want unknown before;
Although the loss that brought us pain,
  That loss but made us love the more,

With further lookings on.   The kiss,
  The woven arms, seem but to be
Weak symbols of the settled bliss,
  The comfort, I have found in thee:
But that God bless thee, dear — who wrought
  Two spirits to one equal mind —
With blessings beyond hope or thought,
  With blessings which no words can find.

                              ALFRED TENNYSON

ALL MOTHER.

IF I had an eagle's wings,
    How grand to sail the sky!
But I should drop to the earth
  If I heard my baby cry.
My baby — my darling,
  The wings may go, for me.

If I were a splendid queen,
  With a crown to keep in place,
Would it do for a little wet mouth
  To rub all over my face?
My baby — my darling,
  The crown may go, for me.

ELIZA SPROAT TURNER.

A GRACE FOR A CHILD.

H ERE, a little child, I stand,
    Heaving up my either hand;
Cold as paddocks though they be,
Here I lift them up to Thee,
For a benison to fall
On our meat, and on us all.   Amen.

ROBERT HERRICK.

THE CHILDREN'S HOUR.

B ETWEEN the dark and the daylight,
    When the night is beginning to lower,
Comes a pause in the day's occupations,
  That is known as the Children's Hour.

I hear in the chamber above me
  The patter of little feet,
The sound of a door that is opened,
  And voices soft and sweet.

From my study I see in the lamplight,
 Descending the broad hall stair,
Grave Alice, and laughing Allegra,
 And Edith with golden hair.

A whisper and then a silence:
 Yet I know by their merry eyes
They are plotting and planning together
 To take me by surprise.

A sudden rush from the stairway,
 A sudden raid from the hall!
By three doors left unguarded
 They enter my castle wall!

They climb up into my turret
 O'er the arms and back of my chair;
If I try to escape, they surround me;
 They seem to be everywhere.

They almost devour me with kisses,
 Their arms about me entwine,
Till I think of the Bishop of Bingen
 In his Mouse-Tower on the Rhine!

Do you think, O blue-eyed banditti,
 Because you have scaled the wall,
Such an old moustache as I am
 Is not a match for you all!

I have you fast in my fortress
 And will not let you depart,
But put you down into the dungeon
 In the round-tower of my heart.

And there will I keep you forever,
 Yes, forever and a day,
Till the walls shall crumble to ruin,
 And moulder in dust away.

HENRY WADSWORTH LONGFELLOW.

THE TOYS.

MY little son, who looked from thoughtful eyes
 And moved and spoke in quiet, grown-up wise,
Having my law the seventh time disobeyed,
I struck him, and dismissed
With hard words and unkissed, —
His mother, who was patient, being dead.
Then, fearing lest his grief should hinder sleep,
I visited his bed;
But found him slumbering deep,
With darkened eyelids, and their lashes yet
From his late sobbing wet.
And I, with moan,
Kissing away his tears, left others of my own;
For on a table drawn beside his head,
He had put within his reach,
A box of counters, and a red-veined stone,
A piece of glass, abraded by the beach,

10

And six or seven shells,
A bottle with blue-bells,
And two French copper coins, ranged there with care-
     ful art,
To comfort his sad heart.
So when that night I prayed
To God, I wept and said :
Ah ! when at last we lie with trancèd breath,
Not vexing Thee in death,
And Thou rememberest of what toys
We made our joys,
How weakly understood
Thy great commanded good,
Then, fatherly, not less
Than I whom Thou hast moulded from the clay,
Thou 'lt leave thy wrath and say :
" I will be sorry for their childishness."

                              COVENTRY PATMORE.

MORNING-GLORY.

WONDROUS interlacement !
          Holding fast to threads by green and
     silky rings,
With the dawn it spreads its white and purple wings ;
Generous in its bloom, and sheltering while it clings,
     Sturdy morning-glory.

     Creeping through the casement,
Slanting to the floor in dusty, shining beams,
Dancing on the door in quick, fantastic gleams,

Comes the new day's light, and pours in tideless
    streams,
  Golden morning-glory.

  In the lowly basement,
Rocking in the sun, the baby's cradle stands;
Now the little one thrusts out his rosy hands;
Soon his eyes will open; then in all the lands
    No such morning-glory.

H. H. JACKSON.

A MOTHER'S PICTURE.

SHE seemed an angel to our infant eyes!
    Once when the glorifying moon revealed
  Her who at evening by our pillow kneeled, —
Soft-voiced and golden-haired, from holy skies
Flown to her loves on wings of Paradise, —
  We looked to see the pinions half-concealed.
  The Tuscan vines and olives will not yield
Her back to me who loved her in this wise,

And since have little known her, but have grown
  To see another mother tenderly
Watch over sleeping children of my own.
Perhaps the years have changed her, yet alone
  This picture lingers; still she seems to me
  The fair young angel of my infancy.

EDMUND CLARENCE STEDMAN.

THE HAPPY CHILD.

TOYS and treats and pleasures pass
    Like a shadow in a glass,
Like the smoke that mounts on high,
Like a noonday's butterfly.

Quick they come and quick they end,
Like the money that I spend;
Some to-day, to-morrow more,
Short, like those that went before.

Mother, fold me to your knees!
How much should I care for these
Little joys that come and go
If you did not love me so?

Father, now my prayer is said,
Lay your hand upon my head!
Pleasures pass from day to day,
But I know that love will stay.

While I sleep it will be near;
I shall wake and find it here;
I shall feel it in the air,
When I say my morning prayer.

And when things are sad or wrong,
Then I know that love is strong;
When I ache or when I weep,
Then I know that love is deep.

Love is old and love is new,
You love me and I love you;
And the Lord who made it thus,
Did it in His love for us.

WILLIAM BRIGHTY RAND.

BABY MINE.

BABY mine, with the grave, grave face,
    Where did you get that royal calm,
Too staid for joy, too still for grace?
   I bend as I kiss your pink, soft palm;
Are you the first of a nobler race,
           Baby mine?

You come from the region of *long ago*,
   And gazing awhile where the seraphs dwell
Has given your face a glory and glow, —
   Of that brighter land have you aught to tell?
I seem to have known it — I more would know,
           Baby mine.

Your calm blue eyes have a far-off reach:
   Look at me now with those wondrous eyes.
Why are we doom'd to the gift of speech
   While you are silent and sweet and wise?
You have much to learn — you have more to teach,
           Baby mine.

FREDERICK LOCKER.

COMPENSATION.

I AM not a prosperous man;
  The ships I send to sea
Are apt to meet some strange defeat
  Ere they come back to me.
And her eyes are dulled with care,
  And the castle that serves our prime
Is a poor affair to those in the air
  We built in our courting time.

This morning, waking slow
  To a sense of the coming day,
Of the life too mean, and the might have been,
  My coward heart gave way.
My heart, appalled, sank down,
  But rose again with a leap
At our delight when at dead of night
  Our babe laughed out in his sleep.

                    ELIZA SPROAT TURNER.

LIKE A LITTLE CHILD.

MY child is lying on my knee,
  The signs of heaven she reads;
My face is all the heaven she sees,
  Is all the heaven she needs.

And she is well, yea, bathed in bliss,
  If heaven is in my face;
Behind it all is tenderness
  And truthfulness and grace.

I mean her well so earnestly,
  Unchanged in changing mood;
My life would go, without a sigh,
  To bring her something good.

I also am a child, and I
  Am ignorant and weak;
I gaze upon the starry sky,
  And then I must not speak,

For all behind the starry sky,
  Behind the world so broad,
Behind men's hearts and souls doth lie
  The Infinite of God.

Ay, true to her, though troubled sore,
  I cannot choose but be;
Thou who art peace forevermore
  Art very true to me.

If I am low and sinful, bring
  More love where need is rife;
Thou knowest what an awful thing
  It is to be a life.

Lo! Lord, I sit in thy wide space,
    My child upon my knee;
She looketh up into my face,
    And I look up to Thee.

                    GEORGE MACDONALD.

TO A CHILD.

IF by any device or knowledge
    The rosebud its beauty could know,
It would stay a rosebud forever,
Nor into its fulness grow.

And if thou could'st know thy own sweetness,
O little one, perfect and sweet!
Thou would'st be a child forever,
Completer whilst incomplete.

                    FRANCIS TURNER PALGRAVE.

THE GOLDEN MILE–STONE.

EACH man's chimney is his golden mile-stone,
    Is the central point from which he measures
            Every distance,
Through the gateways of the world around him.

In his farthest wanderings still he sees it;
Hears the talking flame, the answering night-wind,
            As he heard them
When he sat with those who were, but are not.

Happy he whom neither wealth nor fashion,
Nor the march of the encroaching city,
                    Drives an exile
From the hearth of his ancestral homestead.

We may build more splendid habitations,
Fill our rooms with paintings and with sculptures,
                    But we cannot
Buy with gold the old associations!

                              HENRY WADSWORTH LONGFELLOW.

HOME COMFORT.

AND at night the Septette of Beethoven,
    And grandmother by in her chair,
And the foot of all feet on the sofa
    Beating delicate time to the air.

                              CHARLES KINGSLEY.

WHICH?

"WHICH shall it be?   Which shall it be?"
    I looked at John — John looked at me:
Dear, patient John, who loves me yet
As well as though my locks were jet.
And when I found that I must speak,
My voice seemed strangely low and weak:
"Tell me again what Robert said!"
And then I, listening, bent my head.
"This is his letter:

"'I will give
A house and land while you shall live
If, in return, from out your seven
One child to me for aye is given.'"
I looked at John's old garments worn,
I thought of all that John had borne
Of poverty and work and care,
Which I, though willing, could not share;
I thought of seven mouths to feed,
Of seven little children's need,
And then of this.

"Come, John," said I,
"We'll choose among them as they lie
Asleep." So, walking hand in hand,
Dear John and I surveyed our band.
First to the cradle light we stepped,
Where Lilian the baby slept,
A glory 'gainst the pillow white.
Softly the father stooped to lay
His rough hand down in loving way,
When dream or whisper made her stir,
And huskily he said: "Not her!"

We stooped beside the trundle-bed,
And one long ray of lamplight shed
Athwart the boyish faces there
In sleep so pitiful and fair.

I saw on Jamie's rough red cheek
A tear undried. Ere John could speak,

" He 's but a baby too," said I,
And kissed him as we hurried by.

Pale, patient Robbie's angel face
Still in his sleep bore suffering's trace :
" No, for a thousand crowns, not him,"
He whispered while our eyes were dim.

Poor bad Dick ! our wayward son,
Turbulent, reckless, idle one
Could he be spared ?   Nay, He who gave
Bade us befriend him to the grave ;
Only a mother's heart can be
Patient enough for such as he ;
" And so," said John, " I would not dare
To send him from her bedside prayer."

Then stole we softly up above,
And knelt by Mary, child of love.

" Perhaps for her 't would better be,"
I said to John.   Quite silently
He lifted up a curl that lay
Across her cheek in wilful way,
And shook his head, " Nay, love, not thee,"
The while my heart beat audibly.

Only one more, our eldest lad,
Trusty and truthful, good and glad —
So like his father. " No, John, no —
I cannot, will not let him go."

And so we wrote, in courteous way,
We could not give one child away.
And afterward toil lighter seemed,
Thinking of that of which we dreamed,
Happy in truth that not one face
We missed from its accustomed place;
Thankful to work for all the seven,
Trusting the rest to One in heaven.

ANON.

LAURA, MY DARLING.

LAURA, my darling, the roses have blushed
    At the kiss of the dew, and our chamber is
        hushed;
Our murmuring babe to your bosom has clung,
And hears in his slumber the song that you sung;
I watch you asleep with your arms round him thrown,
Your links of dark tresses wound in with his own.
And the wife is as dear as the gentle young bride
Of the hour when you first, darling, came to my side.

Laura, my darling, our sail down the stream
Of Youth's summers and winters has been like a dream;
Years have but rounded your womanly grace,
And added their spell to the light of your face;
Your soul is the same as though part were not given
To the two, like yourself, sent to bless me from
        heaven, —
Dear lives, springing forth from the life of my life,
To make you more near, darling, mother and wife!

Laura, my darling, there's hazel-eyed Fred,
Asleep in his own tiny cot by the bed,
And little King Arthur, whose curls have the art
Of winding their tendrils so close round my heart;
Yet fairer than either and dearer than both,
Is the true one who gave me in girlhood her troth.
For we, when we mated for evil and good, —
What were we, darling, but babes in the wood?

Laura, my darling, the years which have flown
Brought few of the prizes I pledged to my own.
I said that no sorrow should roughen her way, —
Her life should be cloudless, a long summer's day.
Shadow and sunshine, thistles and flowers,
Which of the two, darling, most have been ours?
Yet to-night, by the smile on your lips, I can see
You are dreaming of me, darling, dreaming of me.

Laura, my darling, the stars that we knew
In our youth are still shining as tender and true;
The midnight is sounding its slumberous bell,
And I come to the one who has loved me so well.
Wake, darling, wake, for my vigil is done:
Who shall dissever our lives which are one?
Say, while the rose listens under her breath,
" Naught until death, darling, naught until death ! "

EDMUND CLARENCE STEDMAN.

THE OLD LOVE SONG.

JUNE 28, 1890.

PLAY it slowly, sing it lowly,
  Old familiar tune !
Once it ran in dance and dimple,
  Like a brook in June ;
Now it sobs along the measures
  With a sound of tears ;
Dear old voices echo through it,
  Vanished with the years.

Play it slowly, — it is holy
  As an evening hymn ;
Morning gladness hushed to sadness
  Fills it to the brim.
Memories home within the music,
  Stealing through the bars,
Thoughts within its quiet spaces
  Rise and set like stars.

Ripple, ripple, goes the love-song
  Till, in slowing time,
Early sweetness grown completeness
  Floods its every rhyme :
Who together learn the music
  Life and death unfold,
Know that love is but beginning
  Until love is old.

Singing, singing through the roses
  Went our lovers twain, —
Was there ever such a rose time,
  Could there be again ?
Now they tell us " Five-and-twenty
  Junes we 've seen them blow ;
Every June 's completer, sweeter, —
  Well we lovers know ! "

WILLIAM C. GANNETT.

HOLIDAYS.

THE holiest of all holidays are those
  Kept by ourselves in silence and apart;
The secret anniversaries of the heart,
When the full river of feeling overflows; —
The happy days unclouded to their close;
  The sudden joys that out of darkness start
  As flames from ashes ; swift desires that dart
Like swallows singing down each wind that blows !
White as the gleam of a receding sail,
  White as a cloud that floats and fades in air,
  White as the whitest lily on a stream,
These tender memories are; — a Fairy Tale
  Of some enchanted land we know not where,
  But lovely as a landscape in a dream.

HENRY WADSWORTH LONGFELLOW.

BETROTHED ANEW.

THE sunlight fills the trembling air,
    And balmy days their guerdons bring;
The Earth again is young and fair,
    And amorous with musky Spring.

The golden nurslings of the May
    In splendor strew the spangled green,
And hours of tender beauty play,
    Entangled where the willows lean.

Mark how the rippled currents flow;
    What lustres on the meadows lie!
And hark, the songsters come and go,
    And trill between the earth and sky.

Who told us that the years had fled,
    Or borne afar our blissful youth?
Such joys are all about us spread,
    We know the whisper was not truth.

The birds, that break from grass and grove,
    Sing every carol that they sung
When first our veins were rich with love,
    And May her mantle round us flung.

O fresh-lit dawn! immortal life!
    O Earth's betrothal, sweet and true,
With whose delights our souls are rife,
    And aye their vernal vows renew!

Then, darling, walk with me this morn,
    Let your brown tresses drink its sheen;
These violets, within them worn,
    Of floral fays shall make you queen.

What though there comes a time of pain
    When autumn winds forebode decay;
The days of love are born again,
    That fabled time is far away!

And never seemed the land so fair
    As now, nor birds such notes to sing,
Since first within your shining hair
    I wove the blossoms of the Spring.

EDMUND CLARENCE STEDMAN.

THE GOOD SISTER.

THERE is no friend like a sister,
    In calm or stormy weather,
To cheer one on the tedious way,
To fetch one if one goes astray,
To lift one if one totters down,
To strengthen whilst one stands.

CHRISTINA G. ROSSETTI.

LOVE AND DEATH.

WHEN the end comes, and we must say good-by
 And I am going to the quiet land;
 And sitting in some loved place hand in hand,
For the last time together, you and I,
We watch the winds blow, and the sunlight lie
 Above the spaces of our garden home,
 Soft by the washing of the western foam,
Where we have lived and loved in days past by, —
We must not weep, my darling, or upbraid
 The quiet death who comes to part us twain ;
 But know that parting would not be such pain
Had not our love a perfect flower been made.
And we shall find it in God's garden laid
 On that sweet day wherein we meet again.

ANON.

BROTHER AND SISTER.

I CANNOT choose but think upon the time
 When our two lives grew like two buds that kiss
At lightest thrill from the bee's swinging chime,
Because the one so near the other is.

He was the elder and a little man
Of forty inches, bound to show no dread,
And I the girl that, puppy-like, now ran,
Now lagged behind my brother's larger tread.

I held him wise, and when he talked to me
Of snakes and birds, and which God loved the best,
I thought his knowledge marked the boundary
Where men grew blind, though angels knew the rest.

Long years have left their writing on my brow,
But yet the freshness and the dew-fed beam
Of those young mornings are about me now,
When we two wandered toward the far-off stream

With rod and line.   Our basket held a store
Baked for us only, and I thought with joy
That I should have my share, though he had more,
Because he was the elder and a boy.

The firmaments of daisies since to me
Have had those mornings in their opening eyes,
The bunchèd cowslip's pale transparency
Carries that sunshine of sweet memories.

Those hours were seed to all my after good;
My infant gladness, through eye, ear, and touch,
Took easily as warmth a various food
To nourish the sweet skill of loving much.

Our brown canal was endless to my thought;
And on its banks I sat in dreamy peace,
Unknowing how the good I loved was wrought,
Untroubled by the fear that it would cease.

Slowly the barges floated into view,
Rounding a grassy hill to me sublime
With some Unknown beyond it, whither flew
The parting cuckoo toward a fresh spring time.

His sorrow was my sorrow, and his joy
Sent little leaps and laughs through all my frame;
My doll seemed lifeless, and no girlish toy
Had any reason when my brother came.

School parted us; we never found again
That childish world where our two spirits mingled
Like scents from varying roses that remain
One sweetness, nor can evermore be singled.

Yet the twin habit of that early time
Lingered for long about the heart and tongue;
We had been natives of one happy clime,
And its dear accent to our utterance clung

Till the dire years whose awful name is Change
Had grasped our souls still yearning in divorce,
And pitiless shaped them in two forms that range
Two elements which sever their life's course.

But were another childhood-world my share,
I would be born a little sister there.

GEORGE ELIOT.

FRIENDSHIP.

A RUDDY drop of manly blood
    The surging sea outweighs;
The world uncertain comes and goes,
The lover rooted stays.
I fancied he was fled,
And after many a year
Glowed unexhausted kindliness,
Like daily sunrise there.
My careful heart was free again:
O friend, my bosom said,
Through thee alone the sky is arched,
Through thee the rose is red;
All things through thee take nobler form,
And look beyond the earth, —
The mill-round of our fate appears
A sun-path in thy worth.
Me too thy nobleness has taught
To master my despair;
The fountains of my hidden life
Are through thy friendship fair.

RALPH WALDO EMERSON.

EXCUSE.

I TOO have suffered.   Yet I know
    She is not cold, though she seems so:
She is not cold, she is not light;
But our ignoble souls lack might.

She smiles, and smiles, and will not sigh,
While we for hopeless passion die;
Yet she could love, those eyes declare,
Were but men nobler than they are.

Eagerly once her gracious ken
Was turned upon the sons of men;
But light the serious visage grew, —
She looked, and smiled, and saw them through.

Our petty souls, our strutting wits,
Our labored, puny passion fits, —
Ah, may she scorn them still, till we
Scorn them as bitterly as she!

Yet O that Fate would let her see
One of some worthier race than we, —
One for whose sake she once might prove
How deeply she who scorns can love!

His eyes be like the starry lights,
His voice like sounds of summer nights!
In all his lovely mien let pierce
The magic of the universe!

And she to him will reach her hand,
And gazing in his eyes will stand,
And know her friend, and weep for glee,
And cry, Long, long I 've looked for thee!

Then will she weep. With smiles till then
Coldly she mocks the sons of men.
Till then her lovely eyes maintain
Their gay, unwavering, deep disdain.

MATTHEW ARNOLD.

OUR TWO OPINIONS.

U S two wuz boys when we fell out, —
    Nigh to the age uv my youngest now ;
Don't rec'lect what 't wuz about,
    Some small deeff'rence, I 'll allow.
Lived next neighbors twenty years,
    A-hatin' each other, me 'nd Jim, —
He havin' *his* opinyin uv *me*,
    'nd *I* havin' *my* opinyin uv *him*.

Grew up together 'nd would n't speak,
    Courted sisters, 'nd marr'd 'em too ;
'Tended same meetin'-house oncet a week,
    A-hatin' each other through and through !
But when Abe Linkern asked the West
    F'r soldiers, we answered, — me 'nd Jim, —
He havin' *his* opinyin uv *me*,
    'nd *I* havin' *my* opinyin uv *him*.

But down in Tennessee one night
    Ther wuz sound uv firin' fur away,
'nd the sergeant allowed ther 'd be a fight
    With the Johnnie Rebs some time nex' day ;

'nd as I wuz thinkin' uv Lizzie 'nd home,
  Jim stood afore me, long 'nd slim, —
He havin' *his* opinyin uv *me*,
  'nd *I* havin' *my* opinyin uv *him*.

Seemed like we knew there wuz goin' to be
  Serious trouble f'r me 'nd him;
Us two shuck hands, did Jim 'nd me,
  But never a word from me or Jim!
He went *his* way 'nd *I* went *mine*,
  'nd into the battle's roar went we, —
I havin' *my* opinyin uv Jim,
  'nd *he* havin' *his* opinyin uv *me*.

Jim never come back from the war again,
  But I haint forgot that last, last night
When, waitin' f'r orders, us two men
  Made up 'nd shuck hands, afore the fight.
'nd after all, it 's soothin' to know
  That here *I* be 'nd yonder 's Jim,
He havin' *his* opinyin uv *me*,
  'nd *I* havin' *my* opinyin uv *him*.

EUGENE FIELD.

NEW HOUSE: OLD HOME.

YOUR house is built on holy ground:
  A loving home was here,
Where I a kindly welcome found
  For many a goodly year.

I bless the old with grateful heart,
  With joy I hail the new,
Whose walls the builder's patient art
  Have built so sound and true.

With happy eyes its strength I see,
  And all its beauty own :
Each part complete as 't were to be
  Prized for itself alone.

New House — Old Home; O happy walls
  For such a glory meet ! —
To echo little children's calls,
  And hear their pattering feet;

To shield them in their gentle sleep,
  Nor frown upon their play;
The treasure of their life to keep
  From every harm away.

Here love that seemed complete before
  Shall yet more perfect grow,
As every happy year shall more
  Of inward grace bestow.

New House ! But still old books shall cheer,
  Old music sway the heart,
And flowers that have been always dear
  Their tender grace impart.

Old Home ! for o'er the threshold strange
   Old friends shall haste to prove
How little changing place can change
   The hearts of those who love.

Old Home! for westering age shall shed
   Its blessing on the scene,
With sacred thoughts that daily wed
   What is with what hath been ;

Ay, and what is with that beyond
   Our vision's farthest scope
Which makes each memory sweet and fond
   A promise and a hope.

New House, Old Home ! and what if here
   An emblem true should be
Of things which shall to us appear
   In love's eternity ?

                              JOHN W. CHADWICK.

AT FOUR–SCORE.

THIS is the house she was born in, full four-score
      years ago, —
And here she is living still, bowed and ailing, but
   clinging
Still to this wonted life, — like an ancient and blasted
   oak-tree
Whose dying roots yet clasp the earth with an iron
   hold.

This is the house she was born in, and yonder across
    the bay
Is the home her lover built, — for her and for him and
    their children;
Daily she watched it grow, from dawn to the evening
    twilight,
As it rose on the orchard hill, 'mid the spring-time
    showers and bloom.

There is the village church, its steeple over the trees
Rises and shows the clock she has watched since the
    day it was started, —
'T is many a year ago, how many she cannot remember:
Now solemnly over the water rings out the evening
    hour.

And there in that very church, — though, alas, how
    bedizened and changed !
They 've painted it up, she says, in their queer, new,
    modern fashion, —
There on a morning in June she gave her hand to her
    husband ;
Her heart it was his (she told him) long years and
    years before.

Now here she sits at the window, gazing out on steeple
    and hill ;
All but the houses have gone, — the church, and the
    trees, and the houses ; —

All, all have gone long since, parents and husband
    and children ;
And herself, — she thinks, at times, she too has van-
    ished and gone.

No, it cannot be she who stood in the church that
    morning in June,
Nor she who felt at her breast the lips of a child in the
    darkness :
But hark ! in the gathering dusk comes a low, quick
    moan of anguish, —
Ah, it is she indeed who has lived, who has loved, and
    lost.

For she thinks of a wintry night when her last was
    taken away, —
Forty years this very month, — the last, the fairest,
    the dearest ;
All gone, — ah, yes, it is she who has loved, who has
    lost and suffered,
She and none other it is, left alone in her sorrow and
    pain.

Still with its sapless roots, that stay though the
    branches have dropped,
Have withered and fallen and gone, their strength and
    their glory forgotten ;
Still with the life that remains, silent and faithful and
    steadfast,
Through sunshine and bending storm clings the oak
    to its mother-earth.

                                    RICHARD WATSON GILDER.

TÊTE-À-TÊTE.

I.

A BIT of ground, a smell of earth,
  A pleasant murmur in the trees,
The chirp of birds, an insect's hum,
  And, kneeling on their chubby knees,

Two neighbors' children at their play ;
  Who has not seen a hundred such ? —
A head of gold, a head of brown,
  Bending together till they touch.

II.

A country schoolhouse by the road,
  A spicy scent of woods anear,
And all the air with summer sounds
  Laden for who may care to hear.

So do not two, a boy and girl,
  Who stay when all the rest are gone,
Solving a problem deeper far
  Than one they seem intent upon.

Dear hearts, of course they do not know
  How near their heads together lean ;
The bee that wanders through the room
  Has hardly space to go between.

III.

Now darker is the head of brown,
    The head of gold is brighter now,
And lines of deeper thought and life
    Are written upon either brow.

The sense that thrilled their being through
    With nameless longings vast and dim,
Has found a voice, has found a name,
    And where he goes she follows him.

Again their heads are bending near,
    And bending down in silent awe
Above a morsel pure and sweet,
    A miracle of love and law.

How often shall their heads be bowed
    With joy or grief, with love and pride,
As waxeth strong that feeble life,
    Or slowly ebbs its falling tide !

IV.

A seaward hill where lie the dead
    In dreamless slumber deep and calm ;
Above their graves the roses bloom,
    And all the air is full of balm.

They do not smell the roses sweet ;
    They do not see the ships that go
Along the far horizon's edge ;
    They do not feel the breezes blow.

Here loving hands have gently laid
  The neighbors' children, girl and boy,
And man and wife ; head close to head
  They sleep, and know nor pain nor joy.

JOHN W. CHADWICK.

TWO LOVERS.

TWO lovers by a moss-grown spring :
  They leaned soft cheeks together there,
  Mingled the dark and sunny hair,
And heard the wooing thrushes sing.
          O budding time !
          O love's blest prime !

Two wedded from the portal stept :
  The bells made happy carollings,
  The air was soft as fanning wings,
White petals on the pathway slept.
          O pure-eyed bride !
          O tender pride !

Two faces o'er a cradle bent :
  Two hands above the head were locked ;
  These pressed each other while they rocked,
Those watched a life that love had sent.
          O solemn hour !
          O hidden power !

Two parents by the evening fire :
   The red light fell about their knees
   On heads that rose by slow degrees
Like buds upon the lily spire.
             O patient life !
             O tender strife !

The two still sat together there,
   The red light shone about their knees;
   But all the heads by slow degrees
Had gone and left that lonely pair.
             O voyage fast !
             O vanished past !

The red light shone upon the floor
   And made the space between them wide ;
   They drew their chairs up side by side,
Their pale cheeks joined, and said, " Once more ! "
             O memories !
             O past that is !

                  GEORGE ELIOT.

IN TWOS.

SOMEWHERE in the world there hide
   Garden-gates that no one sees
Save they come in happy *twos*, —
Not in ones, nor yet in threes.

But from every maiden's door
Leads a pathway straight and true ;
Maps and surveys know it not ;
He who finds, finds room for two !

WOODLAND VOWS.

From painting by Robert Beyschlag.

Then they see the garden-gates !
Never skies so blue as theirs,
Never flowers so many-sweet
As for those who come in pairs.

Round and round the alleys wind :
Now a cradle bars their way,
Now a little mound, behind, —
So the two go through the day.

When no nook in all the lanes
But has heard a song or sigh,
Lo ! another garden-gate
Opens as the two go by !

In they wander, knowing not :
" Five and Twenty ! " fills the air
With a silvery echo low,
All about the startled pair.

Happier yet *these* garden-walks ;
Closer, heart to heart, they lean ;
Stiller, softer falls the light ;
Few the twos, and far between.

Till, at last, as on they pass
Down the paths so well they know
Once again at hidden gates
Stand the two : they enter slow.

12

Golden gates of Fifty Years,
May *our* two your latchet press!
Garden of the Sunset Land,
Hold their dearest happiness.

Then a quiet walk again :
Then a wicket in the wall;
Then one, stepping on alone, —
Then two at the Heart of All!

WILLIAM C. GANNETT.

THE OLD MAN DREAMS.

O FOR one hour of youthful joy!
  Give back my twentieth spring!
I 'd rather laugh, a bright-haired boy,
  Than reign, a gray-beard king.

Off with the spoils of wrinkled age!
  Away with learning's crown!
Tear out life's wisdom-written page,
  And dash its trophies down!

One moment let my life-blood stream
  From boyhood's fount of flame!
Give me one giddy, reeling dream
  Of life all love and fame!

My listening angel heard the prayer,
  And, calmly smiling, said,
" If I but touch thy silvered hair
  Thy hasty wish hath sped.

" But is there nothing in thy track
  To bid thee fondly stay
While the swift seasons hurry back
  To find the wished-for day ? "

" Ah, truest soul of womankind !
  Without thee what were life ?
One bliss I cannot leave behind:
  I 'll take — my — precious — wife ! "

The angel took a sapphire pen
  And wrote in rainbow dew ;
" The man would be a boy again,
  And be a husband too ! "

" And is there nothing yet unsaid,
  Before the change appears ?
Remember, all their gifts have fled
  With those dissolving years."

" Why, yes, for memory would recall
  My fond paternal joys ;
I could not bear to leave them all —
  I 'll take — my — girl — and — boys."

The smiling angel dropped his pen,
  "Why this will never do;
The man would be a boy again,
  And be a father too!"

And so I laughed, — my laughter woke
  The household with its noise,—
And wrote my dream, when morning broke,
  To please the gray-haired boys.

                    OLIVER WENDELL HOLMES.

THE DAISY FOLLOWS SOFT THE SUN.

THE daisy follows soft the sun,
    And when his golden walk is done,
  Sits shyly at his feet.
He, waking, finds the flower near.
"Wherefore, marauder, art thou here?"
  "Because, sir, love is sweet!"

We are the flower, Thou the sun!
Forgive us, if as days decline,
  We nearer steal to Thee,
Enamoured of the parting west,
The peace, the flight, the amethyst,
  Night's possibility!

                    EMILY DICKINSON.

INDEX OF FIRST LINES.